OLYMPIC WEIGHTLIFTING FOR MASTERS

"Do not go gentle into that good night,
Old age should burn and rave at close of day;
Rage, rage against the dying of the light."

—Dylan Thomas

OLYMPIC WEIGHTLIFTING FOR MASTERS

TRAINING AT 30, 40, 50 & BEYOND

By Matt Foreman

Book design by Ryan Scheife / Mayfly Design and typeset in the Albertina MT and TheSans typefaces

ISBN-13 978-0-9800111-8-0

Catalyst Athletics, Inc
www.catalystathletics.com

Catalyst Athletics, Inc and Matt Foreman advise that the exercises and techniques described in this book can be strenuous and may not be appropriate for all individuals, and do not make any claim to the safety of said exercises and techniques. The nutrition information herein exists for example purposes only and in no way represents a prescription for any individual. It is strongly recommended that the reader consult a physician before engaging in any of the activities or practices illustrated or described herein. Catalyst Athletics, Inc and Matt Foreman disclaim any and all liability for any injury sustained or condition arising from the performance of any of the exercises or practice of any of the nutrition ideas described in this book.

This book is dedicated to Norbert Schemansky,
who changed my beliefs about what human beings are capable of

TABLE OF CONTENTS

INTRODUCTION

If you're reading this book, there are a few possibilities:

1. You're an old person.
2. You're not currently an old person, but you will be soon.
3. You coach old people.
4. You're not an old person, but you're interested in them (that sounds weird).

I think that sums up our demographic of readers. You're involved in Olympic weightlifting in some way. Some of you might be coaches, but I imagine the vast majority of you are athletes who want to train and compete in weightlifting and, like we just mentioned, you're old.

To be fair, I think we need to define exactly what an "old person" is. Seriously, where's the cutoff for your youth? Do you become an old person at a certain age? Let me give you a couple of statements I've heard over the years that address this exact question. Back in 1990, I was reading an issue of USA Weightlifting magazine. There was a write-up in this issue about the results of the US Olympic Festival, which used to be one of the main highlights of our national schedule. Anyway, there was a quote in this write-up about Tony Urrutia. Tony won the Festival that year in the old 82.5 kilo weight class (181 lbs) with a 145 kg snatch (319 lbs) and a 182.5 C&J (402 lbs). For those of you who don't know who he was, Tony was a former three-time World Champion from Cuba who defected to the United States in the early 80s. He went through the arduous citizenship process and eventually started competing again as a US lifter. By this time, he was obviously older. He was actually 32 when he won the Festival in 1990. The magazine had a quote from Tony I've never forgotten. He said, "When you're old, it's a lot tougher to win. When you're past 25 years old, you're old."

25? Really? Is that a universally accepted number that separates young people and old people, or was that just the opinion of one particular guy? Well, I've actually heard that same thought from multiple places. When I was gathering ideas for this book, I remembered an old article I read by a highly successful powerlifting coach named Tim McClellan. Tim interviewed some very reputable exercise physiologists about the effects of age on strength athletes, and they universally agreed that 25 is the time when things start to get bumpy for a lifter. One of them was actually quoted as stating, "You start to die at 25. Your body no longer produces hormones at the same rate it did when it was younger."

Okay, so we've got various opinions from experts and they all support the idea that athletes start to go downhill in weightlifting when they pass 25. I imagine that's discouraging for you to read, since the vast majority of you are probably way past that magic number. You're in your 30s, 40s, 50s, or maybe even beyond that, right? You bought this book because you wanted some hope, some encouraging information that helps you believe you've still got a lot of big weightlifting potential despite the fact that you're a developmental crusty geezer, and the first thing you read in the introduction is that you've passed your peak. The experts agree that your best days are already gone, and now your physical potential is spiraling into the crapper.

Listen, I'm intentionally being sarcastic here because I know you're all intelligent people with a realistic outlook on where you're at in life. If you're in your 40s or something like that, you already know that you've passed the young peak years of your athletic experience. Unless you live in some alternate universe of denial and ignorance, I'm not telling you something you don't already understand. You're not a kid anymore, and your body can't do many of the things it used to do.

But you still want to be weightlifters. My guess is that many of you found this sport at a later age. There's a pretty good chance that you were introduced to it through some extension of CrossFit, since that's how almost everybody in this country is discovering Olympic lifting these days. It didn't take you long to get excited about it, I'm sure. This sport is very easy to fall in love with. You know you're not starting at the optimal age. We all know that. However, you still want to do it. It's probably becoming a consuming passion in your life, and you don't really give a damn how old you are. You're emotionally invested at this point, and you're not going to stop.

That's where one of your first problems starts to surface. You see, there's almost no literature floating around the weightlifting world about how to train and compete successfully when you're older. Most of the coaches and researchers in the sport don't really care about older athletes. They're focused on producing world and Olympic champions. That means their efforts are all going to be centered around athletes who start training in their teenage years (or earlier) and reach their peak in their early 20s. That's when you're physically ready for the big time, because your hormones and other physiological qualities are the highest they're ever going to be in your life.

In other words, all of the weightlifting information you've researched doesn't really have much application to you. You're in your 30s, 40s, 50s or whatever, and the only training material you can find is structured for athletes who are 20-30 years younger than you. So what does this mean? Unfortunately, it often leads to older athletes trying to use training programs they found online that are specifically designed for younger athletes. These old lifters are new to the sport and they often don't have much coaching or experience, so they have to resort to the trusty old internet to get some guidance. They follow the only programs they can find, which are not intended for anybody at an advanced age. In short, you've got a 42 year-old weightlifter trying to follow a program that's set up for a 22 year-old weightlifter.

Where does this lead? Many of you know the answer to that question already. It leads to overtraining, injury, and just a general feeling of being beat to hell all the time. I'll bet I just described a large majority of you. Listen, I have a pretty wide circle of acquaintances in weightlifting and I talk to older lifters all the time. Almost every single one of them tells me how beat up they are. Their joints hurt, they're not making progress, and the frustration is starting to really dig into them. Why are these people all so banged up? There are two main reasons:

1. First of all, weightlifting is simply a very difficult sport. Regardless of what age you're at, it's physically grueling.
2. They're overtraining.

Seriously, just back up and think about this for a second. You've got an old person trying to follow the training program of a young person, and the old person's body simply can't keep up with it. It blows my mind how many people these days just can't understand this concept. When you're old, you can't do the things you used to do when you were young. It's one of the simplest ideas in the galaxy, brothers and sisters. And if you try to use a young person's training volume when you're in your 30s or beyond, there's an extremely high chance that your body isn't going to be able to handle it. Presto, you've got an overtrained athlete.

On top of that, many of the coaches who are working with older athletes in this sport have no idea what they're doing. These coaches are often younger people themselves, so they've got absolutely no clue what it feels like to be old. And even if the coaches are older individuals, it's very likely they don't have a lot of personal experience with old weightlifting. If they were athletes themselves, they probably retired at a relatively young age like most people do, so they don't really have a complete grasp of what the body can and can't do in the aging years. Also, their coaching efforts, like the information we found on the internet, is all specifically directed towards young athletes who are trying to make the Olympic Team.

Sadly, there's one more piece of the puzzle that makes your weightlifting endeavors so challenging. Most people just don't give a damn about you. Seriously, they're not interested in what you're doing. When coaches start their careers, they dream of producing Olympians. I don't think I've ever met a coach who said, "You know, I feel a burning passion to help 55 year-old people lift their own bodyweight." The general public is part of this, too. When they watch weightlifting, they want to see massive Russian dudes clean and jerking 500 lbs. Or they want to watch the CrossFit Games and see a half-naked hot chick snatching 185 lbs. Most of the world doesn't want to see lifters with grey hair, loose skin, and sagging breasts trying to split clean 138 lbs. In a nutshell, there aren't a lot of weightlifting resources for old people because nobody cares about them.

I care, brothers and sisters. I'm one of you, for crying out loud. I'm in my 40s now, and my desire to be a weightlifter is just as strong as it was when I started the sport 26 years ago. I know how much this means to you, believe me. And I also know how frustrated most of you are, for the reasons we've just mentioned. That's why I'm writing this book. I want to help. You're going to get a lot of resources in here, and hopefully they'll give you a chance to extend your weightlifting career for as long as you want it to last. You've got goals, and nobody should think they're unimportant. I salute you for having the courage and passion to pursue one of the hardest sports in the world at a time in your life when you don't enjoy the same advantages you had when you were a kid. You deserve respect, and you also deserve legitimate information that will make you better. Those are the fundamental ideas behind this thing.

—Matt Foreman

OVERVIEW OF OLYMPIC WEIGHTLIFTING

Before we start delving into the nitty gritty of this book, we need to make sure we're all on the same page about exactly what Olympic weightlifting is. I'm aware that those of you who are reading this are coming from a variety of backgrounds and experience levels. Some of you have prior involvement in Olympic lifting (extensive, in some cases) and you don't need a beginner's breakdown of the sport. However, some of you decided to read this book because Olympic weightlifting sounds like a really cool new thing to try. You want to learn because you don't know much about it. For those people, we need a basic introduction. For those of you with experience, this will be a quick review of things you already know. Just follow me through it, and we'll start getting to the earth-shattering stuff later.

Weightlifting is the name of an actual sport. Laypeople think of "weightlifting" as a blanket term that covers all manner of training with barbells, dumbbells, etc. That's incorrect. Weightlifting is an Olympic sport where athletes compete against each other in two lifts: the snatch, and the clean & jerk.

These two movements are referred to as "the Olympic lifts." When you go to a weightlifting competition, athletes will perform both of these lifts and attempt to hoist the biggest weights they're capable of. Competitions are won and lost based on the athlete's total, which is simply the added combination of their snatch and clean and jerk weights. In other words, if a weightlifter competes in a contest (which are commonly called *meets*), and he snatches 250 lbs and clean and jerks 325 lbs, his total is 575 lbs (250 + 325 = 575). His 575 lb total will then be matched against the totals of his competitors, and the highest total wins the meet. Weightlifting competitions are divided according to gender, bodyweight classes, and age divisions (We'll take a look at the exact weight classes and age groups later.).

Because weightlifting is an Olympic sport, the most common names for it in the strength world are *Olympic weightlifting, Olympic lifting*, or often just *OLifting*. It's important to know that there are other strength sports with different names, and you don't want to confuse them with each other:

Powerlifting: This is a completely different sport from Olympic weightlifting. In powerlifting, athletes compete in three lifts: the squat, bench press and deadlift.

Strongman: This is also a different sport where athletes compete in a variety of non-traditional events, such as stone lifting, farmer's walk (walking while carrying heavy objects in each hand), pulling heavy objects with a rope, such as cars or buses, and various other skills.

Bodybuilding: This is a sport where athletes use weight training exercises to build their physiques. They compete by posing in front of judges, who determine the winners based on the most aesthetically pleasing muscular appearance.

None of these sports are in the Olympics.

When you have conversations with people who are well-versed and experienced in strength training and competition, they'll usually know the proper terminology and differences between these sports. Saying "I'm a weightlifter" is a specific statement, not a general one. It means you train and compete in Olympic lifting. Saying "I'm a powerlifter" or "I do strongman" identifies those other sports. People who don't know much about this stuff often confuse them. I've told several people over the years that I'm an Olympic lifter, and the first thing they ask is "How much can you bench press?" They're confusing Olympic lifting with powerlifting, where the bench press is one of the competition lifts. Most Olympic weightlifters don't do many of the lifts or events from the other sports in their training, such as bench press or stone lifting from strongman.

Anybody with extensive Olympic lifting experience has had to explain this stuff to people countless times. Most people who go to a 24-Hour-Fitness-type gym and start working out on weight machines will go to work and tell their friends, "I do weightlifting" even though they aren't Olympic lifters. They're not saying this because they're stupid or anything. They simply aren't familiar with all the exact elements of competitive strength sports. These are common mistakes in terminology that happen all the time.

Some people like to do a variety of lifts and exercises from the various sports. They'll do snatch, clean and jerk, but also bench press, deadlift, and maybe some stone lifting. These people are sometimes referred to as *strength generalists,* because they don't confine their training to any specific sport. They like to do a little of everything, a general mix. Sometimes they compete in one (or all) of these sports, enjoying the variety and diversity.

This book, as we mentioned, is specifically focused on Olympic weightlifting. The other strength sports will not be substantial elements in here. OLifting is one of the oldest sports in the world, and it has massive international participation from almost every country on the planet that has any kind of athletic program.

The Olympic lifts (snatch and clean & jerk) are extremely technical, complex movements that require high levels of strength, quickness, balance, flexibility, agility, and coordination. For most people, they're hard to learn and developing real expertise takes a long time. They are total body movements meaning they don't isolate any one specific muscle group of the body the way a dumbbell curl in bodybuilding would isolate the bicep muscles, for example. The Olympic lifts demand a substantial amount of work from every single part of the body. For this exact reason, the snatch and clean & jerk are popular lifts with athletes in various sports. It's not uncommon for coaches to include the Olympic lifts in the weight training programs used by football players, wrestlers, track athletes, etc. because these lifts greatly improve an athlete's overall strength and physical capability.

The Olympic lifts are very difficult, but they're also quite easy to get addicted to. Because of their technical nature, they present an interesting challenge to athletes. Once people try them, they're usually hooked. I think one of the main reasons for the addictive element of the Olympic lifts is the incredible feeling of accomplishment that comes from performing them with skill and precision. Here are some sequence photos of what the Olympic lifts look like:

The snatch

The clean & jerk

You don't know how lucky you are to live in the age of the internet. Many of you didn't even need those sequence photos because you've already explored YouTube and found enough Olympic lifting videos to keep you busy for years. It's a great way to learn about the sport, and anybody who's serious about this business should be maximizing the resources of the internet. When you watch these videos, you see some amazing feats of strength performed by athletes who are a lot younger than you, correct? These Olympic champions and record breakers are in the young, prime years of their lives. If you're reading this book, you've got a little more mileage than they do. So now that you've got a little information about the basic terminology and essentials of weightlifting, we should probably transition into looking at the potential you have to do this sport in your not-a-spring-chicken-anymore years.

SECTION ONE

Addressing Prior Notions of Age in Weightlifting

Masters Weightlifting: Questions and Facts

The information you're going to get in this book is intended to be practical and useful. We're going to provide you with ideas about training programs, injury and pain management, learning progressions, recovery methods, and several other areas. Weightlifting is a very physical sport, so you're going to read quite a bit about the physical things you need to do for success.

However, there's also an enormously important mental aspect to all of this. If you've got any experience in weightlifting whatsoever, you've already learned that it's a mind game. I think it gets even trickier as the years go by and you pass into the phase of life we're talking about here. This sport requires considerable levels of strength, power, speed, agility, flexibility, and kinesthetic awareness. These are the qualities that start to diminish as we age. This shouldn't be a news flash to you since it's a basic biological fact. However, the decrease in your physical abilities is what leads to an even tougher mental challenge, because you start to ask yourself a lot of questions when you think about being a weightlifter in your older years:

"Is it POSSIBLE for me to lift successfully when I'm old?"

"Is it SAFE to lift when I'm old?"

"Am I going to get any SATISFACTION from the results I produce when I'm old, knowing that they'll most likely be lower than what I produced when I was young?"

"Am I setting myself up for HEALTH PROBLEMS if I try to continue such a demanding sport when I'm old?"

"I've never done this before, so IS THERE ANY POINT in trying to learn such complicated athletic skills when I'm already physically limited because of my age?"

These thoughts pop into your mind when you ponder the journey as an older weightlifter, and they're all totally legitimate. First of all, the general public sees weightlifting as a dangerous bone-snapping slaughterhouse where your knee joints will spontaneously detonate as soon as you squat down below parallel with a barbell in your hands. How many times have you been around an average Joe who saw Olympic lifting on TV and said, "Ooohhh! That looks really dangerous!" It's a pretty common reaction, and it's annoying because most of these people have no hesitation about letting their kids join football or soccer teams, which are two sports that have dramatically higher injury rates than weightlifting does. It's just a lack of understanding, plain and simple. People think this sport is ridiculously risky, and it's actually much safer than many mainstream sports. That's been statistically proven.

Let me give you some facts and figures that support this point. In Olympic weightlifting (and many other sports), athletes who are 35 years old or older are classified as *masters*. From now on, we'll be using the term *masters* frequently, instead of just saying "old athletes." In weightlifting, the masters division is separated by 5-year increments. In other words, the age groups are set up like this:

35-39 years old	55-59 years old	75-79 years old
40-44 years old	60-64 years old	80-84 years old
45-49 years old	65-69 years old	85-89 years old
50-54 years old	70-74 years old	90-94 years old

(At the international level, anyone over 80 is often simply classified in the "80 + age group." But USA national competitions include the 85-89 and, when necessary, the 90-94 age groups.)

Right away, I know what you're thinking. "Why in the hell are there age groups for 85-89 years old, and for 90-94?! Nobody is still competing in Olympic weightlifting at that age!" And you would be wrong, my friend. If you go online and check the USA Masters Weightlifting website (www.mastersweightlifting.org), you can click on the USA National Records section and you'll find a complete set of American record lifts in the men's 85-89 age group. Believe it or not, there are multiple athletes who are still getting on the platform and competing after their 80th birthdays.

Want to hear a funny story? I was at a national masters meet a few years ago and I bumped into an old guy in the hotel elevator who was competing in the 85-89 division. I asked him, "So what are you going to do after you finish competing tomorrow? Get some rest and relaxation?" He said, "Hell no! I'm gonna take some Viagara and go downtown looking for broads!" Seriously, that's what he said.

Here are some statistics from the 2013 World Masters Weightlifting Championships held in Turin, Italy. I want to show you how many lifters competed in this contest. I've broken it down by age groups, with the total number of competitors listed below.

2013 World Masters Weightlifting Championships

Women's Division	**Men's Division**
35-39 age group: 22 athletes	35-39 age group: 39 athletes
40-44 age group: 29 athletes	40-44 age group: 47 athletes
45-49 age group: 25 athletes	45-49 age group: 52 athletes
50-54 age group: 12 athletes	50-54 age group: 47 athletes
55-59 age group: 11 athletes	55-59 age group: 41 athletes
60-64 age group: 9 athletes	60-64 age group: 49 athletes
65-69 age group: 9 athletes	65-69 age group: 39 athletes
70-74 age group: 1 athlete	70-74 age group: 22 athletes
Total participation: 118 athletes	75-79 age group: 32 athletes
	80 + age group: 17 athletes
	Total participation- 385 athletes

Total combined participation: 503 athletes

See what I'm talking about? Masters weightlifting is a global activity, and a lot of people are doing it. 503 athletes, age 35 and above, lifted in this meet. In case you don't know much about the sport, 503 entries in one contest is an enormous turnout. Also, you need to keep a couple of facts in mind:

> This was a World Championship, so the only people who were allowed to compete were those who met the qualifying standards. Just like any international weightlifting meet, there were qualifying weights that athletes had to lift in their respective national championships before they were eligible to compete at the world level.
>
> As we mentioned, the competition was held in Turin, Italy. Obviously that means it was a long, expensive trip for athletes who were traveling from overseas or the far reaches of Europe and Asia. This tells us that there are obviously a lot of masters athletes around the world who didn't come to the meet, simply because of the travel factors.
>
> These two factors leave us with the clear conclusion that the large participation at this contest represents only a small fraction of the active masters weightlifters in the world. To state it simply, there are tons of old people who are still doing this sport.

So let's get back to a few of those questions you were asking, and let's start the book with some answers:

Question: *"Is it POSSIBLE for me to lift successfully when I'm old?"*

Answer: Obviously YES. There are hundreds of people competing at the highest international level of masters weightlifting, which means there are thousands of others doing it at the lower levels.

Question: *"Is it SAFE to lift when I'm old?"*

Answer: Obviously YES. These people all trained safely for this meet, showed up, competed, and then went home healthy. It's not like they were evacuated from the platform in ambulances (or hearses). Apparently, some of them even got jacked up on Viagara and went out looking to get laid afterwards. So the physical danger associated with weightlifting is, like the report of Mark Twain's death, greatly exaggerated.

Question: *"Am I going to get any SATISFACTION from the results I produce when I'm old, knowing that they'll most likely be lower than what I produced when I was young?"*

Answer: Obviously YES. The people who lifted in this meet traveled to Italy from countries all over the world. Do you think they would have sacrificed that much time and money for something unfulfilling, discouraging, or boring? Trust me, the satisfaction of this sport, even at the masters level, is thrilling and addicting.

Question: *"Am I setting myself up for HEALTH PROBLEMS if I try to continue such a demanding sport when I'm old?"*

Answer: Obviously NO. Do you want to know how we get that answer? Look back at the breakdown of athletes in the various age groups of the Worlds. In the men's division, there were more competitors between the ages of 60-69 than there were in the 35-44 age range. So it's not like you only get a few more good years out of yourself when you pass the 35 mark and then everything collapses right away. Many athletes are still going strong in their mid/late 60s, for crying out loud. Did weightlifting give them health problems? No! They wouldn't be competing if that were the case.

Important Note: At this point, you might be wondering about something. The title of this book indicates that we're addressing people starting at 30 years old, and we just said the youngest age for a master is 35. If you're reading this and you're 31 or 32, don't think this doesn't apply to you. You're close enough, trust me. We'll mention masters classifications quite a bit, but it doesn't mean you're in an entirely different category if you're around 30. Having been 30 myself, I can positively verify that when I was that age, I was already starting to feel some of the things we're going to talk about in this book. I just threw this disclaimer in here so you don't think this book is only for people who are officially in the masters division.

Masters World Records: The Facts About What's Physically Possible

Now we've established an important point. It should be clear to you that Olympic weightlifting is entirely possible at an advanced age, and we're not just talking about your 40s. The worldwide popularity of masters lifting is a great way to prove that a big accumulation of birthdays doesn't have to stop you from doing any of this stuff. To state it simply...if lots of other people are doing it, you can probably do it too.

However, let's take this a few steps further. We now understand that it's possible to continue the sport as a master. But you're all wondering about something else. Here's another situation where I can read your mind and see the question you're asking:

> *"Okay, I know that I can still lift weights when I'm old. But I'm probably not going to be able to lift BIG weights when I'm old. What's the point in lifting as a master if I'm going to be stuck doing piddly little weights that don't impress anybody?"*

This is a completely reasonable point. I think it's especially true for people who were formerly great athletes in their younger years. If you've got an Olympic champion who snatched a world record 400 lbs when he was 24, how much fun is he going to have snatching 200 lbs when he's 55? Won't that seem like a humiliating step down in performance?

Let me give you a personal perspective on that. When I was doing my lifetime-best lifting back in the 90s, I had lifts of 155 kg in the snatch (341 lbs) and 185 kg in the clean and jerk (407 lbs). I was one of the top-ranked athletes in the United States in my weight class. Back then, I used to see masters lifters competing at local meets and wonder to myself, "Why the hell would anybody want to still be lifting when they know they're never gonna beat their all-time top lifts because they're too old?" Like all young people, I just didn't see a point in it. It seemed stupid to accept such a big drop-off in performance.

Fast-forward fifteen years. Last year (2013), I competed in a local meet and snatched 127 kilos (280 lbs). I was 40 years old at the time. Brothers and sisters, I can tell you without any hesitation that it was still thrilling and totally gratifying to get out there on the platform and hit a 280 snatch at 40, even though that weight was 61 lbs below my lifetime personal record. Trust me, masters lifting is a lot more fun than it looks. I think many of the athletes from my age group have no interest in masters competition, and I totally understand. It's not for everybody. Still, I discovered something about myself—and this sport—when I decided to extend my career past my prime years. Even when you know you've already passed your peak, it's still a kick in the ass to get on the platform and battle the barbell. I didn't know that when I was a kid, but I know it now.

Now let's take the focus back to you, and what's possible in your elder years. Here is a list of the IWF world weightlifting records in the masters division. Please notice that I didn't include the records for every age group, simply to avoid taking up several pages of this book. I think we can make our point by just giving you samples of various masters age group records. So I'm giving you the records for the age groups 35-39, 45-49, 55-59, etc. and skipping the groups in between, such as 40-44, 50-54, etc. If you want to examine the records I didn't include here, please feel free to do so. They're easy to locate on the USA Masters Weightlifting website I mentioned earlier at www.mastersweightlifting.org. You can see a complete list under the Records section. But as I said, here's a glimpse of the top all-time performances by older weightlifters around the world. I didn't include the names of the record holders, but the actual weights are all accurate.

You might already know this, but Olympic weightlifting is broken down into bodyweight classes as well as age groups:

Men's Weight Classes	**Women's Weight Classes**
56 kg (123 lbs)	48 kg (105 lbs)
62 kg (136 lbs)	53 kg (116 lbs)
69 kg (152 lbs)	58 kg (128 lbs)
77 kg (169 lbs)	63 kg (138 lbs)
85 kg (187 lbs)	69 kg (152 lbs)
94 kg (208 lbs)	75 kg (165 lbs)
105 kg (231 lbs)	+75 (over 165 lbs)
+105 (above 231 lbs)	

Obviously you can apply these classes to yourself to figure out where you would compete, and how you measure up against the best. So, check these records out:

Current IWF World Records, Masters Division (as of May 2014), Men's Division

35-39 age group

BODYWEIGHT CLASS	SNATCH	CLEAN & JERK	TOTAL
56 kg (123 lbs)	93 kg (205 lbs)	117.5 kg (259 lbs)	202.5 kg (446 lbs)
62 kg (136 lbs)	118 kg (260 lbs)	147 kg (324 lbs)	262 kg (576 lbs)
69 kg (152 lbs)	124 kg (273 lbs)	160 kg (352 lbs)	280 (617 lbs)
77 kg (169 lbs)	140.5 kg (309 lbs)	175 kg (385 lbs)	315 kg (694 lbs)
85 kg (187 lbs)	145 kg (319 lbs)	176 kg (387 lbs)	320 kg (705 lbs)
94 kg (208 lbs)	155 kg (341 lbs)	182.5 kg (402 lbs)	332.5 kg (733 lbs)
105 kg (231 lbs)	153 kg (337 lbs)	191 kg (420 lbs)	343 kg (755 lbs)
+105 kg (over 231 lbs)	173 kg (380 lbs)	203 kg (447 lbs)	374 kg (823 lbs)

45-49 age group

BODYWEIGHT CLASS	SNATCH	CLEAN & JERK	TOTAL
56 kg (123 lbs)	89 kg (196 lbs)	109 kg (240 lbs)	198 kg (436 lbs)
62 kg (136 lbs)	96 kg (211 lbs)	117 kg (258 lbs)	210 kg (462 lbs)
69 kg (152 lbs)	115 kg (253 lbs)	135 kg (297 lbs)	250 (551 lbs)
77 kg (169 lbs)	122 kg (269 lbs)	147.5 kg (325 lbs)	260 kg (573 lbs)
85 kg (187 lbs)	126 kg (277 lbs)	148.5 kg (327 lbs)	267 kg (587 lbs)
94 kg (208 lbs)	131 kg (288 lbs)	166 kg (365 lbs)	290 kg (638 lbs)
105 kg (231 lbs)	140 kg (308 lbs)	171 kg (376 lbs)	307 kg (676 lbs)
+105 kg (over 231 lbs)	143 kg (315 lbs)	180.5 kg (397 lbs)	320 kg (705 lbs)

55-59 age group

BODYWEIGHT CLASS	SNATCH	CLEAN & JERK	TOTAL
56 kg (123 lbs)	75 kg (165 lbs)	90 kg (198 lbs)	160 kg (352 lbs)
62 kg (136 lbs)	84 kg (185 lbs)	103.5 kg (227 lbs)	185 kg (407 lbs)
69 kg (152 lbs)	100 kg (220 lbs)	120.5 kg (265 lbs)	215 (473 lbs)
77 kg (169 lbs)	107.5 kg (237 lbs)	128 kg (282 lbs)	227.5 kg (501 lbs)
85 kg (187 lbs)	108 kg (238 lbs)	135 kg (297 lbs)	240 kg (529 lbs)
94 kg (208 lbs)	123 kg (271 lbs)	152.5 kg (336 lbs)	275 kg (606 lbs)
105 kg (231 lbs)	122.5 kg (270 lbs)	151 kg (332 lbs)	270 kg (595 lbs)
+105 kg (over 231 lbs)	122 kg (269 lbs)	146 kg (321 lbs)	257 kg (566 lbs)

65-69 age group

BODYWEIGHT CLASS	SNATCH	CLEAN & JERK	TOTAL
56 kg (123 lbs)	60 kg (132 lbs)	73 kg (161 lbs)	132.5 kg (292 lbs)
62 kg (136 lbs)	71 kg (156 lbs)	91 kg (210 lbs)	160 kg (352 lbs)
69 kg (152 lbs)	83 kg (182 lbs)	103 kg (226 lbs)	180 (396 lbs)
77 kg (169 lbs)	93 kg (205 lbs)	117 kg (258 lbs)	205 kg (451 lbs)
85 kg (187 lbs)	94 kg (208 lbs)	118 kg (260 lbs)	209 kg (460 lbs)
94 kg (208 lbs)	98 kg (215 lbs)	126 kg (277 lbs)	224 kg (494 lbs)
105 kg (231 lbs)	104 kg (229 lbs)	130 kg (286 lbs)	234 kg (516 lbs)
+105 kg (over 231 lbs)	96 kg (211 lbs)	122 kg (269 lbs)	218 kg (480 lbs)

75-79 age group

BODYWEIGHT CLASS	SNATCH	CLEAN & JERK	TOTAL
56 kg (123 lbs)	51 kg (112 lbs)	61 kg (134 lbs)	110 kg (242 lbs)
62 kg (136 lbs)	58 kg (128 lbs)	73 kg (161 lbs)	131 kg (288 lbs)
69 kg (152 lbs)	65 kg (143 lbs)	82 kg (180 lbs)	147 (324 lbs)
77 kg (169 lbs)	72.5 kg (160 lbs)	90 kg (198 lbs)	158 kg (348 lbs)
85 kg (187 lbs)	78 kg (171 lbs)	95 kg (209 lbs)	173 kg (381 lbs)
94 kg (208 lbs)	75 kg (165 lbs)	93 kg (205 lbs)	167 kg (369 lbs)
105 kg (231 lbs)	80 kg (176 lbs)	100 kg (220 lbs)	180 kg (396 lbs)
+105 kg (over 231 lbs)	66 kg (145 lbs)	84 kg (185 lbs)	150 kg (330 lbs)

Current IWF World Records, Masters Division (as of May 2014), Women's Division

35-39 age group

BODYWEIGHT CLASS	SNATCH	CLEAN & JERK	TOTAL
48 kg (105 lbs)	60 kg (132 lbs)	73 kg (161 lbs)	132.5 kg (292 lbs)
53 kg (116 lbs)	65 kg (143 lbs)	82 kg (180 lbs)	147 kg (324 lbs)
58 kg (128 lbs)	70 kg (154 lbs)	95 kg (209 lbs)	165 kg (363 lbs)
63 kg (138 lbs)	71 kg (156 lbs)	95 kg (209 lbs)	165 kg (363 lbs)
69 kg (152 lbs)	73 kg (161 lbs)	97 kg (213 lbs)	167 kg (369 lbs)
75 kg (165 lbs)	81 kg (178 lbs)	98 kg (215 lbs)	177 kg (390 lbs)
+75 (over 165 lbs)	96 kg (211 lbs)	125 kg (275 lbs)	220 kg (485 lbs)

45-49 age group

BODYWEIGHT CLASS	SNATCH	CLEAN & JERK	TOTAL
48 kg (105 lbs)	52.5 kg (115 lbs)	62.5 kg (137 lbs)	115 kg (253 lbs)
53 kg (116 lbs)	57.5 kg (127 lbs)	71 kg (156 lbs)	126 kg (277 lbs)
58 kg (128 lbs)	65 kg (143 lbs)	78 kg (171 lbs)	142.5 kg (314 lbs)
63 kg (138 lbs)	68 kg (149 lbs)	82 kg (180 lbs)	150 kg (330 lbs)
69 kg (152 lbs)	64 kg (141 lbs)	87.5 kg (192 lbs)	150 kg (330 lbs)
75 kg (165 lbs)	68 kg (149 lbs)	83 kg (182 lbs)	150 kg (330 lbs)
+75 (over 165 lbs)	78 kg (171 lbs)	99 kg (218 lbs)	177 kg (390 lbs)

55-59 age group

BODYWEIGHT CLASS	SNATCH	CLEAN & JERK	TOTAL
48 kg (105 lbs)	32 kg (70 lbs)	38 kg (83 lbs)	68 kg (149 lbs)
53 kg (116 lbs)	45 kg (99 lbs)	57 kg (126 lbs)	101 kg (222 lbs)
58 kg (128 lbs)	51 kg (112 lbs)	62 kg (136 lbs)	113 kg (249 lbs)
63 kg (138 lbs)	45 kg (99 lbs)	58 kg (128 lbs)	102 kg (224 lbs)
69 kg (152 lbs)	50 kg (110 lbs)	68 kg (149 lbs)	118 kg (260 lbs)
75 kg (165 lbs)	57 kg (142 lbs)	77 kg (169 lbs)	134 kg (295 lbs)
+75 (over 165 lbs)	55 kg (121 lbs)	67 kg (147 lbs)	122 kg (269 lbs)

65-69 age group

BODYWEIGHT CLASS	SNATCH	CLEAN & JERK	TOTAL
48 kg (105 lbs)	23 kg (50 lbs)	31 kg (68 lbs)	54 kg (119 lbs)
53 kg (116 lbs)	28 kg (61 lbs)	40 kg (88 lbs)	66 kg (145 lbs)
58 kg (128 lbs)	31 kg (68 lbs)	43 kg (94 lbs)	74 kg (163 lbs)
63 kg (138 lbs)	40 kg (88 lbs)	51 kg (112 lbs)	91 kg (200 lbs)
69 kg (152 lbs)	38 kg (83 lbs)	53 kg (116 lbs)	91 kg (200 lbs)
75 kg (165 lbs)	37 kg (82 lbs)	46 kg (101 lbs)	82 kg (180 lbs)
+75 (over 165 lbs)	37 kg (82 lbs)	48 kg (105 lbs)	81 kg (178 lbs)

WHEW! I know that was a lot of numbers, and you probably didn't check every single one on there. That's why I want to highlight a few random ones, and let's just think about them for a second.

> In the men's 45-49 age group, an athlete in the 77 kg bodyweight class (169 lbs) clean and jerked 147.5 kg (325 lbs). That means this dude almost did a double-bodyweight C&J when he was nearing 50 years of age.
>
> A 105 kilo (231 lb) male athlete in the 65-69 age group did a 130 kg (286 lb) clean and jerk. 65-69 years old, people. This guy was old enough to collect Social Security and qualify for Medicare, and he damn near lifted 300 lbs over his head.
>
> Somewhere between 55 and 59 years of age, a 94 kilo man (208 lbs) snatched 123 kg (271 lbs). I'm a pretty good weightlifter, and I can barely snatch 123 right now at 118 kg bodyweight...and 41 years old.
>
> A woman between the ages of 45 and 49 nailed an 87.5 kg clean and jerk (192 lbs) at 69 kilo bodyweight (152 lbs). Let me tell you something, people. I teach weightlifting at a CrossFit gym, and I've got 150 lb guys who are in their 20s, their prime strength years, and they can't C&J 192 lbs.
>
> Some 55 year-old grandma snatched 51 kg (112 lbs) at only 58 kg (128 lbs) bodyweight. Oh wait, sorry. I stand corrected; she was in the 55-59 age group. So she might have been older than 55. Once again, some of the gals I coach weigh more than 128 and they can't snatch 112...and they're half the grandma's age.

These are phenomenal feats of strength, brothers and sisters. They're simply incredible. Let's stop and think about some of the people we know who are the same age as the record holders I just wrote about. Think about the old geriatrics you see in the airport, towing their little suitcases behind them with their pants pulled up to their armpits. Visualize the geezers at Denny's, pissing and moaning at the hostess because they aren't being seated fast enough. Or think about your 55 year-old dad with his flabby gut, making grunts and groaning noises every time he hoists his fat ass up from his recliner. We're talking about people in this demographic, the ones who look like they're barely strong enough to carry their groceries in from the car. Yeah, you know exactly who I mean. Now imagine those people on a weightlifting platform, competing in one of the most demanding sports in the world. And if you want to really get your mind blown, think about them lifting more weight than you can do right now.

Some of you are in your 30s, just past the peak of your athletic years. You bought this book because you wanted inspiration and resources as you get started with your masters career. Okay, take a look at the 35-39 age group records. A guy in that group snatched 140.5 at 77 bodyweight (that's 309 @ 169). A 58 kilo woman (128 lbs) did a 95 kg clean and jerk (209 lbs).

I'll say it again: these lifts are insane in the brain. I hope you don't think I put them in here to humiliate or discourage you. That's not the intention. I understand many of you are competitive and ambitious, and you might have just seen some record lifts that you'll probably never be able to contend with. Right? Wrong, hopefully. You shouldn't look at records like this and get disheartened. It's actually supposed to be the opposite of that.

The list of records you just saw should be one of the most hope-inspiring motivators of your career. Think about it. Those numbers tell you that amazing feats are possible, for all of us. Do you have the potential to break any of those records? I don't know. Maybe, maybe not. But let's say you embark on a masters career and, somewhere down the road, you hit a lift that's somewhere in the ballpark of these records. Let's say you're a man and you eventually snatch 100 kilos (220 lbs) in the 77 kg class (169 lbs) when you're 58. That lift won't beat the world record (which is 107.5 kg), but think about the athletic accomplishment of being able to snatch that much weight at that age. You could walk into several gyms in the world and beat most of the 77 kilo lifters in the place with a 100 kilo snatch, and they'll be guys who are in their 20s. I can't think of any finer way to grow old, personally.

There's a reason why I used this kind of information to convince you that it's physically possible to be successful in this sport in your old age. I didn't choose to start with a bunch of clinical research and scientific jargon. I'm not dismissing that type of data, because it's enormously important in furthering the human race and improving the quality of our lives. But when I ask myself, "Is something possible?" I like to follow up with a second question, "Well, has it ever been done before? If it's been done, it must be possible." Seeing actual people who have continued their weightlifting careers into the masters years is a simple way of telling us something…

IT CAN BE DONE.

Basic Physiology: A Necessary Concession

Now you're all fired up, correct? We showed you that there are huge possibilities as a masters weightlifter, and you feel like you've got a second shot at greatness ahead of you. Sensational!

However, it's important to shift into a slightly different gear and take a gander at something else. I just mentioned at the end of the last section that I wasn't going to weigh you down by leading into this journey with clinical research about the aging process. Well... Even though I didn't want that stuff to be the first impression you get about masters weightlifting, we actually need to cover some of it, for a couple of reasons. First, it's important that we understand what's going to happen to our bodies as we grow old. When you looked at that list of records, there was an obvious (and understandable) decline as the age groups progressed. People in the 45-49 age group were stronger than people in the 65-69 age group. That wasn't shocking to any of you, because you already have a basic understanding about the physical effects of age. We're going to acknowledge those effects and discuss them because, as I said, you need to know what's going to happen to you...and all of us.

Second, I think we need to know that this isn't going to be as easy as I probably made it sound earlier. When we look at amazing records from older lifters and the large participation in masters weightlifting, we can get carried away with the thought that it's a piece of cake. Knowing that a lot of people do it very successfully can lead to a mentality of, "Hell, this will be no problem!" There are some good things about that mentality, but it would be foolish to go charging into this thing without a complete comprehension of what you're up against, and the tough changes you're not going to be able to get away from.

Biological/medical information and facts:

Most of the research in the field of human physiology agrees that testosterone reaches its peak during the adolescent and early adult years. It's a natural fact of the aging process. Testosterone, for those of you who fell asleep during freshman biology, is the hormone in your body that's primarily responsible for the development of muscle mass and strength. It also plays a large part in bone growth, aggression, and general athletic ass-kicking capabilities. Men have a lot more of it than women. That's just the way our bodies are made. If you read a lot of studies about how much your testosterone drops as you age, you'll find some slightly differing numbers and percentages. But much of the general consensus is that a man's testosterone level starts to decline by 1% per year after he passes 30. That sounds like a major bummer, doesn't it? If you're like me, you instantly start doing calculations in your head when you read a statement like that, trying to predict just how weak and pathetic you're going to be when you're 50.

Testosterone research always seems to be more focused on men, which is logical because it's primarily considered the dominant male sex hormone. Women produce it too, but people are usually a lot less concerned with how testosterone decline impacts the ladies. However, this is a weightlifting discussion, so we need to cover it. Basically, it works in a very similar way as men. The peak of a woman's testosterone level usually hits around the 20s, and then drops to half of that by the time they're in their 40s. It's not an earth-shattering revelation. Women have more complex responses to the drop in testosterone and how drastically it impacts their sex drive and energy levels. Like women themselves, it's very complicated and men have almost no interest in trying to figure it out. Suffice to say that all of us, guys and dolls, are fighting the same basic battle against Father Time.

The physical effects of testosterone decline are pretty easy to understand. Essentially, it's a weakening in all the things that make us so turbocharged when we're young. When guys are in their late teens and 20s, they've got a lot of strength, energy, aggression, and enough sex drive to detonate a nuclear generator. They've also got more muscle mass and lower bodyfat. They haven't started to lose their hair yet and they don't show any signs of becoming an old person. Then, as the years pass after 30, everything starts to gradually slide downhill. Eventually, they're walking around on a golf course with man boobs, grey hair, plaid pants and a rotten attitude because they're so pissed off at being old.

Women also know about how the aging process works, all too well. It's harder to keep the bodyfat off, the boobies hang lower and lower, wrinkly skin, varicose veins, etc. And like men, they often become mean as a snake because they're so bitter about all of it.

Testosterone decrease also contributes to your muscles getting smaller. We've all got different kinds of muscle fiber in our bodies, Type I and Type II. Type I is what's called "slow twitch" muscle fiber, and it contributes to endurance-type activity (stuff that happens relatively slowly, get it?). Type II muscle fibers are called "fast twitch" and they're the ones that make you strong, powerful, explosive, and awesome. In other words, fast twitch muscle fiber is extremely important for weightlifters. And as you get older, the mass of your fast twitch muscles starts to naturally decrease. Isn't that wonderful news? Losing the horsepower of your fast twitch fiber can also cause a loss of agility, coordination, overall body control, etc. That's why old people fall down all the time.

So, the entire athletic quality of your body drops as you get older. News flash, right? Just kidding. Anybody with any understanding of human existence knows that age decreases your physical abilities, and that's why we didn't need this part of the book to be a lengthy scientific dissertation about statistics, levels, cellular activity, etc. To make a long story short, we simply need to acknowledge what we're up against and admit that we're not going to be able to escape any of it.

Personal perspective: I'll throw in some of my own experience and observation about all of this. I'm about to turn 42, so I've glimpsed the future. And let me make a comment to the geezers who are getting revved up right now and saying, "42?! Hell, that ain't nothing! I'm 54, sonny boy! Wait 'til you get to be my age, then see how you feel!!" Hey, Grandpa Moses...I know 42 isn't terribly old yet, and I've still got a long way to go. So settle down, go watch *Murder, She Wrote* and let me finish what I was saying.

I can definitely feel the difference of age, no doubt about it. I'm nowhere near as strong as I used to be. I'm a little flabbier than I was in my 20s, but I've been able to keep it from getting out of control by paying a lot more attention to nutrition than I used to. Remember when we could eat whatever we wanted, and it wouldn't affect us at all? Yeah, those days go bye-bye. Being older, I notice the effects of bad eating a lot more than I used to. When I was young, I could eat nothing but pizza, burritos, ice cream and Cinnabon, and it wouldn't bother me at all. My stomach was like a rock and my training was going to be solid, regardless of how much garbage I gobbled. If I tried that now, I would be chained to my toilet for three days. My joints would also feel a lot puffier and stiff from all the grease and sodium.

Drinking beer is different, too. I know many of you aren't drinkers, but I am. Nowadays, there's a pretty noticeable difference in my recovery time after I get hammered. Twenty years ago, it had almost no impact on my performance at all. Now, it takes me a good two days to really feel normal again if I drink more than three or four.

In other words, all that stuff they say about getting old is true. You don't really think about it when you're young, and you probably shouldn't. But when it finally hits you, there's no evading it. You have to confront it, because it transitions into the next area of concern...getting hurt.

Injury increase

It should be clear that athletes are more susceptible to injuries when they get older. I wish it weren't like this, but it is. For many people, their reaction time decreases as they age. This can be caused by several factors, including a decrease in the amount of blood that flows into the brain. Circulation can also diminish with age, which is why muscles and joints take so much longer to warm up and get loose in masters athletes. Anybody who has done any kind of physical activity when they're older can testify to this. You sometimes hear aging athletes talk about how it takes "an hour to warm up, and then thirty minutes to train." In the simplest terms possible, your body just doesn't get activated as quickly when you're older. Consequently, many of us dive in and start our workouts before our bodies are really prepared. All of the sudden... SNAP! You've got a pulled muscle. This is one example of how you can learn a lot about the physical effects of aging without reading books. Real-life experience teaches you a great deal.

Joint flexibility is a major issue as well. Weightlifting is a sport with a high demand for flexibility, and it's another one of those things you lose when you get older. Cartilage wears away with repeated use over time. Conditions like arthritis and bursitis can start to set in. Connective tissue (tendons and ligaments) start to get stiffer because, as we said, they're not getting as much blood flow as they used to. Doing snatches and clean and jerks with compromised flexibility is difficult, and it makes the chance for injury higher.

Injuries are scary. Nobody wants to get one, especially a really bad one that might require surgery or something like that. However, it's important to mention that your risk for injury can be drastically reduced simply by being more careful and precise about how you take care of your body. An effective warm-up does wonders for your health, as does post-workout stretching. Knowing your body's limits and not getting carried away can add 20 years to your career. Nutrition, as we mentioned earlier, is paramount. Your muscles won't recover properly if you're constantly trying to replenish them with oil, grease, and sugar. Consuming the right amounts of protein and nutrients will make more difference when you're old than you can possibly imagine.

Personal perspective: I've had plenty of injuries. Most of the ones I dealt with throughout my younger years were just the normal stuff like muscle pulls, strains, spasms, tendonitis, etc. These are part of the game if you're a weightlifter, no matter what age you are. These are what we consider "minor injuries" because they don't require surgery or any severe repair measures.

Almost all of them can be fixed with rest and basic treatment procedures like ice, massage, etc.

The big injuries? Well, those are different. I've had two ACL reconstruction surgeries (left and right knees). I had the first one when I was 39, and the injury was the result of a Highland Games throwing accident. I got the second one when I was 41. Interestingly, this one was from a lifting injury that happened 14 years earlier. It was a freak accident, foot slippage on a heavy jerk attempt, one of those things that happens once in a million times. Even though my ACL was torn, I continued lifting on it for years. I finally decided to get it fixed, and both of my knees have fully recovered. I'm still lifting successfully with no residual problems from the injuries.

I refuse to disillusion anybody about the physical risk of weightlifting. You can get hurt doing this stuff. It would be dishonest to say otherwise. Now, it's important to understand that weightlifting has been statistically proven to be much safer than many other sports. It's also crucial to know that your risk of injury can be greatly reduced by proper technique and sensible training. But at the end of the day, it's still a very physical sport with some danger involved.

I competed for 23 years before I had to have any kind of surgery. I know many weightlifters who have never had one at all, period. So there's a high probability that you'll go all the way through your weightlifting career without ever having to go under the knife, or anything close to it. Is there more risk as you get older? Sure there is. But that's where we need to shift the analysis in another direction. We've looked at how the factors of age are going to impact all of us, right? Now we need to take a look at you personally, and how this whole journey is going to pan out for you.

Different Bodies, Common Decisions...

I want to make two points. These are probably two of the most important things I'm going to say in this book, and I want to use a couple of stories to illustrate them.

First, let me tell you about something I saw nine years ago. Obviously this book is about weightlifting. However, I've had a lot of experience in the sport of track and field as well. I've been a track coach for eighteen years, and I've also competed in the masters division in the throwing events (shot put and discus). Back in 2005, I was at a masters track meet in Phoenix. The discus competition was being held on a big field that was about a hundred yards away from the track, and there was a six-foot fence separating them. To get to the discus field, you had to walk to the end of the track stadium, across a small parking lot, through a gate in the fence, and then all the way back across another field to the disc ring. It was about a ten-minute walk, which was a total pain in the ass because it was also over 100 degrees that day. Most of the disc throwers weren't doing any track events, so we just stayed on the field by the ring. However, there were some other athletes who were doing both running and throwing events, which means they had to make that long death march back and forth between the two areas.

This was a masters meet, as I said, so everybody was over 35 and quite a few of the competitors were in their 50s, 60s, or older. Track and field is even more popular with masters than weightlifting is, so there are always big turnouts at these things. Anyway, I was spending the day by the disc ring, waiting for my age group's turn to compete. Some of the older groups were going first, so I saw a lot of their throws. When the 40-44 age group was competing, I noticed one guy in particular. This poor dude looked like he was about to fall apart. He was groaning in pain when he reached down to the ground to pick up his disc, for crying out loud. He walked like somebody was sticking an ice pick in his lower back, his throws looked terrible, and he walked out of the ring after each attempt rubbing his shoulder and hip with a twisted grimace on his face. He didn't look like he was walking away from a disc throw attempt. He looked like he was walking away from a gnarly car accident. And he was between the ages of 40 and 44.

Then I saw something I'll never forget. Off in the distance, I could see a couple of masters who were leaving the track to come to the disc ring. As I said, it was a very long walk to get from one place to the other. Both of these masters were approaching the fence, and I could see they didn't know where the gate opening was. They stopped at the fence and looked right and left, trying to figure out how to get through the thing. Finally, one of them (an older man) pointed down towards the gate, which was about fifty yards away from where they were standing. He shook his head in disgust, but then he turned and walked towards it so he could go through and get to the disc field.

However, the other person he was walking with was an older lady. I actually knew who she was from seeing her around at meets, and I think she was in the 60-64 age group at this time. Apparently, she didn't want to walk all the way down to the gate, because she tossed her bag over the six-foot fence and then proceeded to just climb right over the damn thing. I couldn't believe my eyes. This 60 year-old lady just climbed to the top of this fence and then hopped down to the other side, picking up her bag and heading to the disc ring. And she went over that fence like she was thirteen years old, by the way. It was like watching something from one of those American Ninja Warrior shows on TV. I'm telling you something...I don't know if I could have gone over that fence as easy as she did.

Compare the two people I just told you about. One of them was in his early 40s, and the signs of aging were written all over him like carvings on a petrified tree. Every time he did anything physical, it was accompanied by achy noises and gestures. He was obviously in pain and his performance was a disaster. Then, think about that lady. She was at least twenty years older than the guy, and she hopped a six-foot fence the way a monkey scales the wall of his cage in the zoo. It was effortless, no signs of pain or injury whatsoever. (By the way, I talked to this lady later and found out she was competing in three events that day...the 100 meter dash, the discus, and the pole vault. That's right, folks. A 60 year-old lady doing the pole vault.)

This story is an illustration of the first point I want to make clear to you: *Everybody will have a different physical experience as they get older.* Some people will be achy and ragged by the time they're in their 40s, and others will still be spry and bouncy when they're in their 60s. We're all different, plain and simple. Sure, the physical changes we're going to experience are universal. Nobody is superhuman and our biology is basically the same. We're all gonna die someday, folks. But the impact of age is highly individualized.

If you think about it, this is something we see every day. We all know older people, and we've seen plenty of fluctuations in their physical condition. Some of them are disease-ridden and ready to collapse when they're in their 60s, while others are still skittering around their houses without a care in the world, doing their own yard work and carrying their own luggage on vacation. Which one of those will you be? I don't know. That's between you and Mother Nature. Genetics have a huge role in this, and we can't change the hand we're dealt at birth. There are many things you can do that will make the age process more cooperative with your weightlifting career, and those are the things we're going to delve into with this book. However, the first main point we want to establish is that we're all different, and that's an important fact to know when you think about your future.

For the second point I want to establish, we'll need to look at another story. Actually, this "story" is something that happened in a movie. So it's fictional, but it's one of the best learning moments I've ever seen.

We're talking about the Star Wars series. Specifically, we're talking about *The Empire Strikes Back*. You remember it, right? If you haven't seen the Star Wars movies, there are two things I need to say. First of all, shame on you. Second of all, it'll be okay because I can explain this in a way that makes sense regardless of whether you've seen it or not.

In *The Empire Strikes Back*, a young warrior named Luke Skywalker travels to a foreign planet to learn the ways of the Force from a Jedi master named Yoda. Yoda is the oldest and most powerful Jedi master in the universe, and Luke wants to become stronger by training with him. At one point in the film, the two are training in a dark, desolate swamp area. Luke sees a scary looking cave in the swamp, and he wants to go in there. He feels something inside his mind that's pulling him towards the cave, but not in a good way. It's a mysterious, dangerous feeling in his gut. He feels like he needs to go into the cave so he can find out what's in there. He's not sure what's waiting for him, nor is he sure that he'll be able to come back out alive.

He decides to go into the cave. If you've seen the movie, you know what he finds in there. If you haven't seen it, I'm not going to tell you because you need to be punished for not seeing *The Empire Strikes Back*. Besides, what happens when he walks into the cave has nothing to do with what we're talking about regarding your masters weightlifting career. You see, the part of the story we need to focus on is Luke's decision to enter the cave in the first place. He was at a crossroads moment in his life. There was something inside his soul that was pulling at him. He had a feeling, an urge that he couldn't get rid of. And he knew there was danger involved. He had no idea what was waiting for him in the blackness of that cave, but something in his mind told him it was risky. See where I'm going with this?

He had to make a decision, just like you're going to have to make a decision about whether or not you're going to continue your pursuit of weightlifting into your older years. If you decide to quit, nobody will think less of you. Being an Olympic weightlifter is extremely difficult. Doing it in your masters years is even more difficult because your body wants to stop you. If you choose to walk away and live your life without this sport, that's fair enough. The last time I checked, there's no law written in any bible that says you HAVE to be a weightlifter. If it's not for you... it's not for you.

However, most of you are reading this book because you don't want to walk away. You're interested in being a weightlifter as you get older. Perhaps some of you are still on the fence about it. You know the desire is there, but you're not sure if you really want to go through with this. Brothers and sisters, you're in the same position as Luke Skywalker as he stood at the mouth of that cave. You have to make a decision. After all the analysis and thinking is done, you have to make a choice... move forward or back away. And if you choose to pursue this thing, you have to make a commitment if you expect to be successful.

Some of you might not care much about being competitive. Some of you might not want to compete at all. You may want to simply dabble in this. As far as I'm concerned, that's fine. I don't think there's anything wrong with doing this sport on a limited basis for low-stress recreation. If it makes you happy and makes your life better, more power to you.

On the other hand, some of you might decide to push this thing a little harder. You might want to compete. Hell, you might want to see if you can make a run at winning a masters national championship, or maybe even a world title. If this is the direction you want to go, you'll need a won't-take-no-for-an-answer mentality. Failure can't be an option. If you've got obstacles in your way, life becomes mainly about beating them. If you experience setbacks, you view them as temporary.

At some point, we all just have to walk into the cave. It's a little scary. We know there's risk. But if you've got something inside you that wants to take a shot at this, I think you should do it. If you back away from it, you might spend several years wishing you would have taken the chance and wondering, "What might have been?" I've never been interested in living my life that way, and I have a feeling you're a lot like me.

Want to hear something funny? Look at the fourth sentence of the previous paragraph. It says, *"But if you've got something inside you that wants to take a shot at this, I think you should do it."* Originally, I wrote that sentence as *"But if you've got something inside you that wants to take a shot at this, I think you should* at least give it a try." After I wrote it, I had to go back and revise it because of something I remembered about the word "try." In the movie, there's another scene where Yoda asks Luke to do something difficult. Luke says, "I'll try." If you've seen the movie, you know Yoda's next line. It's the reason I had to change my sentence, and it's the attitude you'll have to take if you want to be a masters weightlifter: *"Do, or do not. There is no try."*

SECTION TWO

Physical Assessment, Prior Training, and Injury History

Training Background

From this point forward, we're going to operate under the assumption that you've made the decision to "walk into the cave" and commit to your masters weightlifting career.

One of the things that makes this situation so interesting is the fact that you're older, which means you've already lived a lot of life. If you think about it, most of the best weightlifters in the world were started in the sport when they were in their early teens or, in many cases, earlier than that. In China, it's normal for children to start weightlifting training in a sports academy when they're 5 or 6 years old. Really! These kids come into the sport with no prior experience of any kind. They've literally been bred into it, almost from birth.

You, on the other hand, have been walking around this planet for 30, 40, or 50 years. That means you've had a variety of experiences. Since we're talking weightlifting, we need to specifically focus on the kind of athletic/physical activity background you're bringing to the table. I've found that most lifters fall into some common categories, and you can plug yourself into the one you belong in:

People who come into masters weightlifting with almost no athletic background whatsoever. Maybe they played T-ball or youth soccer 25 years ago, but that's about it. For all practical purposes, they've got no experience as an athlete.

People who come into masters weightlifting with prior experience from a non-lifting sport (or maybe multiple sports). These are the ones who have a wide background in something like cycling, triathlon, judo, volleyball, etc. They've been serious athletes before, but actual weightlifting training wasn't a big part of it.

People who come into masters weightlifting from another strength sport. Simple...these are the ones who have already done powerlifting, strongman, or bodybuilding. They've got extensive experience with the barbell, but not with Olympic lifting movements.

People who don't really "come into masters weightlifting" because they've been Olympic lifters since they were young. They've got a lot of OL experience, and they simply want to keep it going into their older years.

(By the way, you saw that abbreviation "OL" I just used, right? That stands for "Olympic lifting." We'll be using it a lot throughout the rest of the book, so I just wanted to make sure you know what it means.)

So, which category fits you? I've met masters lifters from every one of these brackets. Interestingly, I haven't really found that any one of them has much of an advantage over any of the others. It might seem like one group, like the former OLifters, is always going to dominate another group, like the "no athletic experience" group, but it doesn't always work that way. At the end of the day, I think age is the great equalizer. But anyway, let's take a look at these groups again, along with the benefits and drawbacks of each one.

No Athletic Background

Benefits

- No bad habits that have to be "unlearned" from other areas.
- Lower chance of prior injuries that could hinder OL training.
- It's easier to teach these people because they're starting from a clean slate.

Drawbacks

- No comprehension of basic athletic qualities (balance, how to jump, how to squat).
- Poor overall muscle development.
- Possible difficulty dealing with pain and soreness (Like many regular people, they think they're injured and need to go to the hospital when they get sore).

Prior Experience from a Non-Lifting Sport

Benefits

- Prior background in general athleticism.
- Understanding of the training process.
- Some strength development.
- Experience in dealing with pain and soreness.

Drawbacks

- Possible prior wear and tear on the body (or pre-existing injuries).
- Mental difficulty in making the transition from "experienced veteran" in another sport to "complete newbie" in OL.
- Constantly comparing OL to their prior sport in ways that don't make sense.

Prior Experience in Another Strength Sport

Benefits

- Obviously, strength development will be present.
- Some understanding of pain management.
- Probably some basic familiarity with OL because of involvement in a closely related field.

Drawbacks

- The athletes want to "muscle" the OL movements when they're learning them, instead of focusing on technique.
- Ego issues: 700 lb deadlifters who have difficulty handling the fact that they can't immediately dominate OL.
- Athletes can be hard to coach because they think they already know everything.

- Probable lack of flexibility.

Prior Experience as Olympic Weightlifters

Benefits

- Obvious advantage in the skill development of the OL movements.
- Little need for instruction or teaching.
- High understanding of all aspects of the sport.

Drawbacks

- Mental transition: Difficulty accepting the decline in a previously high level of performance.
- Frustration as the sport becomes more difficult than it used to be.
- Reluctance (or refusal) to change the way they trained when they were younger.
- They think they know it all already.

As I mentioned earlier, it's hard to make one big blanket prediction for how successful somebody will be as a masters weightlifter, regardless of their prior athletic life (or lack of one). I've seen a wide range of experiences. There are two or three masters competitors I know right now who came from no athletic background whatsoever, and they've both risen to the top of their divisions at the National Masters Championships after a few years of training. They walked into this thing with no prior skills, but they happened to have talent and ability that developed quickly. You have to remember that we're not talking about making the Olympic Team or anything. If you're in your 40s or 50s and you think you're going to make it to the Olympics, I'm sorry to be the one to tell you that you have an unrealistic outlook on where you're at in life. You should be setting different goals for yourself, and one of the biggest ones should simply be to continue training and competing...period.

Obviously there are some examples of athletes who were the best in the country back in their prime years, and are still the best in the country (or world) as masters. Fred Lowe is a good example of this. Fred was an Olympian and multi-national champion back in the 70s, and he has also re-written the record books and won several national titles as a master.

However, I've noticed that most of the best masters lifters in the world weren't superstars when they were young. Many times, they're the kind of athletes who were second or third level national competitors, not the top dogs. I think most of the top-dog lifters who reached the greatest heights in their prime years, such as winning a world title or competing at the Olympics, have less interest in continuing on as masters. They've already made it to the big time, so they (often) simply don't feel the desire to stay with it when they're done with their day in the sun. Plus, many lifters at this level trained in a more professional setting. In other countries, the best lifters are part of a government-funded sports system. Weightlifting is their job, and they do it to put food on the table. The stress and strain of training at this level is extreme, and many of them simply want to walk away and be done with it when they retire. Totally understandable, in my opinion. These people have paid their dues.

The weightlifters who succeed as masters are sometimes the ones who were successful competitors back in the day, but not really the top 1% types. They're the ones who were "middle of the pack" national lifters in their heyday. For whatever reason, people in this bracket seem to keep their desire and motivation to lift longer than others. It might be a feeling that they never really fulfilled their potential, and they want to try to win a world title, come hell or high water, even if it's against a bunch of 63 year-olds. Or maybe they never really burned out the way the elite lifters did, and therefore never developed distaste for training. They never looked at weightlifting and said, "I can't wait to be done with this crap. I'm sick of it." Obviously, these descriptions I'm giving are generalizations. There are some athletes who don't completely fit with any of the categories I'm talking about, and you might be one of them. But taking a wide view of the masses, these are the things I've noticed.

Regardless, your history in sports (and just life in general) will have something to do with the results you ultimately produce as a masters lifter. Finding out where you're at, in terms of your physical health, is a necessary first step in the process.

Injury and Physical History

Because weightlifting is such a physically challenging sport, a person's physical status is going to have a big impact on training and performance. There's a kind of checklist you can implement with yourself, and the goal is finding out if you have any restrictions or complications that are going to hinder your ability to lift when you're old.

Injury History

Have you experienced injuries in the past? If so, which parts of your body were affected? The snatch and clean and jerk are total-body movements, so everything from your head to your toes will be important when you do them. The body parts that you mainly need to look at are:

- Knees
- Shoulders
- Wrists
- Elbows
- Lower back

If you've got a clean bill of health in each of these areas, you've got an immediate advantage over most people and you should be happy about it. If you've had an injury to one of these areas (or any area, really), you need to answer a few questions:

> Has the damage from the injury been repaired? For example: if you tore the meniscus in your knee playing soccer several years ago, did you ever get it surgically fixed?
>
> If you've had surgery, what did your doctor tell you about the long-term physical ramifications of the surgery? Are you going to be permanently limited in your physical capabilities? Or did you get a 100% "all clear" when it was over, with no lasting hindrances?
>
> If you didn't have surgery to repair your injury, do you have any legitimate input from a doctor or physical therapist about what you'll be able to do safely? For example, let's say you have a torn ligament in your knee that you never got repaired. When you lift weights, it doesn't really give you any pain and it's not holding you back from training, but you still know it's torn. Has a qualified expert physician talked to you and told you what the risks are if you continue to lift weights with the torn ligament? Is there a chance that you could make something worse, or injure yourself more? Is something eventually going to snap when you're in the middle of a heavy lift?

If you have an existing injury before you get started with masters weightlifting, you could be rolling the dice with your long-term health. My strong advice would be to consult a doctor who has extensive experience working with athletes. If you visit a general practitioner and say, "I've got a torn ligament in my knee, but I want to continue with Olympic weightlifting," that doctor will probably say something like, "Well, squatting is bad for your knees anyway, so you should just use machines from now on if you want to lift weights." Trust me folks, you can waste a lot of time and money with doctors who have no understanding of what we do.

When you talk to the doctor, get specific answers to specific questions:

- Do I need to get this injury surgically repaired?
- If I get surgery, what are my chances for full recovery?
- How long will the recovery take?
- Will I still be able to lift weights (Olympic weightlifting) after I get the surgery?
- If I don't have surgery, what kind of physical risks am I taking?
- If I don't have surgery, is there anything else I can do (physical therapy, etc.) to keep this injury from getting any worse?

If you don't have any actual injuries, are there any other physical complications that could get in the way of your aspirations as a masters lifter?

- Do you have asthma?
- Are you anemic?
- Do you have chronic problems with things like high blood pressure, heart problems, etc?

We're basically just talking about making sure you're healthy enough to do this sport. If you have any problems like the ones we've just mentioned, it's important to know that you probably still have a legitimate shot at being a masters weightlifter. There are very few physical obstacles that will completely erase your ability to do this. Now, some of your health problems might have an impact on how successful you are. We need to admit that. If you've had some kind of terrible car accident in the past and you've got metal rods in your ankles that severely limit your flexibility, it will affect your ability to do the OLifts. It might create a situation where you can't really sit all the way down into a deep bottom position, maybe permanently.

That might stop you from breaking one of those world records we looked at earlier. But will it stop you from being an OLifter, period? No, it doesn't have to be that way. You'll probably have to modify the SN and C&J (those are abbreviations for snatch and clean and jerk, by the way) movements to accommodate what you're physically capable of. We're going to delve into this concept later, but I'm basically talking about things like this: If you physically can't sit down in a full bottom position, you might have to just do power snatches and power cleans instead.

If you limit yourself to power snatches and power cleans, are you going to make the Olympic Team or break a masters world record? Probably not. But as we said earlier, you shouldn't be hung up on those things anyway.

Doing power snatches and power cleans isn't illegal in competition. If you go to the Masters National Championships, you'll see several athletes doing them. It's not a perfect situation, but it's a hell of a lot better than not being able to do this at all, right?

That last point is an important one to hang on to. I'm talking about the idea that being a masters weightlifter might force you to improvise, adapt, and overcome at some point. Let me give you a personal example of this. Like most weightlifters, I used the split jerk throughout most of my career. The best C&Js of my life were all done with split jerks. Then, in 1999, I had a pretty bad knee injury. When I recovered from it and started lifting again, I couldn't do split jerks effectively anymore. The injury limited my ability in the movement. I could split jerk, but not with any significant weight. And I spent over a year trying to rehab it. I really put in the time and effort to get it back, and I just couldn't make it happen. At first, I thought this was the end of the road. You can't be an OLifter without doing the C&J, right? It's one of the required competition lifts, for Pete's sake.

In my mind, I had two choices:

1. Quit weightlifting
2. Switch to the power jerk (non-split jerk movement) and just do the best I could.

So I switched to the power jerk, knowing that I would probably never be able to match the same results I had with the split jerk.

Was it a perfect situation? No.

Did it limit the amount of weight I was able to lift in the C&J? A little bit.

Did it force me out of weightlifting? **NO.**

To my way of thinking, it would be better to continue on as a weightlifter, even if it meant a slightly lower level of performance. In other words, I would rather do this with some limits than not do it at all. Now, you'll have to make up your mind whether that mentality works for you. If you can't swallow it, maybe you need to step back and ask yourself some more questions. But if you really want to continue as a masters weightlifter, there's probably a strong chance that you'll have to accept a step down at some point. The world record numbers we looked at aren't lying to you. You'll go downhill as you age. But ask yourself the question I just described. Will you be happier lifting smaller weights, or would you rather not lift at all?

When we look at your injury history, we're really talking about addressing any possible limits you might have. If you don't have any at all, hallelujah. You've got a leg up, so enjoy it. But if you've been banged up in the past and your body isn't the same as it used to be, you need to ask yourself a question. Is your injury going to END your weightlifting, or is it going to LIMIT your weightlifting? One of those means you're finished. The other one means you've still got some fight left in you.

Additional personal notes: I mentioned earlier that I tore the ACL in my left knee in 1999, correct? Okay, now let's say something about an ACL tear. For those of you who don't have much athletic experience or knowledge of anatomy, your ACL (anterior cruciate ligament) is one of the most important ligaments in your knee. When it tears, it's a big deal. I can remember being a football player in high school and hearing about ACL tears. Back then, they were basically a death sentence. If a player tore his ACL, it was probably the end of the road. The surgery was brutal, the recovery was long, and the athlete was never the same afterwards. That's what I learned about this particular injury when I was a teenager, and I held on to that understanding all the way into my adult years.

Needless to say, I was terrified when I found out my ACL was torn. I was so terrified, in fact, I didn't even admit to myself that it was true. I denied it. As I said, I continued lifting after 1999 without any surgical repair. Then, in 2011, I finally took the plunge and got it fixed. Let me give you a few details about what happened between the injury and the surgery:

1999 The injury occurred (ACL tear)

2000 I competed in the World University Championships.

2002-3 I dabbled in powerlifting, squatting 714 lbs and deadlifting 672.

2004 I made a comeback in OLifting and qualified for the 2004 Olympic Trials, where I snatched 145 kg (319 lbs) and clean and jerked 172.5 kg (380 lbs).

2008 As a 36 year-old master lifter, I snatched 138 kg (303 lbs) and did a 165 kg C&J (363 lbs).

2011 Six months before my surgery, I deadlifted 600 lbs at 38 years old.

Summer 2011 ACL reconstruction surgery

In other words, everything I did between 1999 and 2011 was done with a complete ACL tear. I'm not telling you this to brag about how tough I am. I'm telling you this because you need to know that injuries can be overcome. Your body is capable of much more than most people think. If you've got something in your body that's damaged or not in 100% tip-top shape, don't think it's going to prohibit you from being a weightlifter.

Don't misunderstand what I'm saying. I'm not telling you that you should start jumping under heavy cleans and snatches if you've got structural damage to your body. As I said in the beginning of this section, you should get some official input from a qualified medical expert if you've got a pre-existing injury. If they tell you that it's unsafe to lift weights with the injury you've got, then you need to look at options for repairing the injury. Don't recklessly charge into weightlifting if there's guaranteed danger involved.

All I'm trying to establish is that there are still great possibilities for what you can do as a masters lifter, even if you've got problematic issues. Additionally, I want to address the old-school beliefs about surgery and recovery. For some reason, I think many people from older generations have grown up thinking of surgery as something that permanently changes you for the worse. Many of you are older, which means you probably grew up with the same views. We think surgery is a bad thing, and you're damaged goods forever after it's over. Well, the thing I learned after getting two ACL reconstructions is that surgery can be a blessing. I recovered from both of my surgeries quickly. The physical therapy process was extremely encouraging and productive, and my knees feel terrific now. I don't have permanent problems. In fact, it's the opposite. I'm in better shape now than I was when I was in my early 30s. Surgery FIXES you, it doesn't HURT you. Obviously that statement largely depends on the type of surgery and the doctor who performs it, but medical science has come a long way in the last 10-20-30 years. Simply put, most surgeries just aren't as brutal as they used to be.

Okay, I'm going to stop talking about surgeries and move on. You might be a little freaked out at this point because you're reading this book to find out more about masters weightlifting and I just gave you four pages about severe injuries and operations. At first glance, that might sound like we're guaranteeing you'll have to deal with this stuff at some point. Not true, brothers and sisters. The vast majority of you will make it through this thing clean as a whistle. The statistics back up that fact. You'll most likely never have a major injury, just minor ones that can be handled without drastic measures. However, it's a fact of life that bad things can happen, and a significant number of you might be coming into this sport with prior damage from something outside of weightlifting. You're older, which makes it a legitimate possibility. That means we needed to talk about it frankly. This book would be irresponsible and incomplete otherwise. Got it? Good.

A Change in Your Mentality

At this point, it should be obvious that we're trying to use this book to change the way you think. Many of you need that change, because the things you've always believed about old age and physical potential are skewed.

What do I mean by that? Well, let's look at an example. As we've discussed, the general public is typically going to shy away from the idea of old people lifting heavy weights. Hell, they're going to shy away from YOUNG people lifting heavy weights, in many cases. But when we think about older people, there's this general notion that it's inherently dangerous to stay athletic and physically active. Right?

Now let's switch our thought patterns for a second. I want you to think about some of the old people you see in your regular life. Visualize airports, restaurants, grocery stores, and other places where it's common to see older people roaming the earth. I want you to think about how so many of them are in bad physical shape. Know what I mean? Some of them walk with canes. Some of them can't walk at all anymore, and they have to be pushed around in wheelchairs or drive one of those little motorized scooters. The ones that can walk often look like hell. They've got bad posture, and they look like they're in pain all the time.

You know what most of these people have in common? The vast majority of them never attempted to lift weights or do anything athletic in their older years. They've been avoiding all that dangerous sports business since they were in their 20s, or maybe even since they graduated high school. What we're saying is that these people stayed away from athletics and lifting weights because they thought it would lead to health problems as they got older. And guess what happened? They got the health problems anyway. I know three older people who have had complete knee replacements within the last few years (including my mother) and every single one of them has lived a sedentary, non-physical life for decades. It's funny, isn't it? We avoid things like weightlifting as we get older because we think they'll give us long-term health problems, and then those health problems wind up happening anyway, often to people who had no real physical activity in their lives. These people watch weightlifting on TV and say to themselves, "Good lord! I would break my hip if I tried that!" And then they still wind up having to get a hip replacement...from doing nothing.

I think people are changing their opinions about age as time progresses. Let me give you another example. Remember when I told you about my experience in track and field? As I mentioned, masters track and field is even more popular than masters weightlifting. Want to hear some of the freakiest old-person athletic feats in the world? A man named Payton Jordan, who was the coach of the US Olympic Track and Field Team in 1968, set a masters world record in the 200 meter dash of 30.89 seconds in the 80-84 age group in 1997. Seriously folks. I couldn't run the 200 in 30 seconds right now, at 41. Most of you probably couldn't either. Jordan did it at 80. Also in track and field, a shot putter from Italy named Mario Riboni set a world record of 5.50 meters (around 18 feet) in 2013...when he was 100. That's right, 100 years old and he's still competing in track meets.

Thousands and thousands of men and women are making different decisions about their old age, and how they want to sail into the sunset. Because you're reading this book, I know you're one of them. There are obviously some very candid conversations we need to have about things like injuries and potential limitations. But I'll keep going back to something I said earlier...these things are limitations, not eliminators. This journey doesn't have to be over if you don't want it to be over.

SECTION THREE

Coaching and Learning

Is Coaching Necessary at Your Age?

Hopefully, we've established at this point that your body isn't going to snap in half or spontaneously detonate when you embark on your weightlifting career as an old person. Now that you know you're on safe ground to begin, we need to look at the issue of getting coached. I started this section with a question: "Is coaching necessary, at your age?" Let me explain what I mean by that. We understand that weightlifting is a very complicated sport, and working with somebody who can teach and train you correctly is extremely important. However, you're not a bunch of 17 year-old kids. You're at a different stage of life, and that's why we need to look at this question in a slightly different way. Let's break down the question and its answers based on who we're talking to.

If you're brand new, or even relatively new to this sport, the answer to the question is absolutely positively YES. However, what you need from a coach is pretty specific, so I need to get back to this point later.

If you're an experienced weightlifter and you're getting into your older years, the answer to the question is MAYBE, MAYBE NOT.

Masters weightlifters with prior experience: Let's say you've been doing this sport for a substantial amount of time. You've got a pretty solid understanding of technique, training, and how to prepare for competition. Hell, you might even be on the upper end of the weightlifting knowledge scale, meaning your grasp of the sport is probably stronger than many of the coaches floating around out there.

Depending on your personality, you might not need to be coached anymore. Some people have independent dispositions, and they don't want to have their hand held every step of the way when they're going about their business. Some adults have developed decision-maker identities, and they're not crazy about the idea of placing themselves as subordinates to anybody. If you've got somebody with a self-regulating personality like this and they want to be a weightlifter, you need to look at a few things:

> If you're old and self-reliant, but you don't know jack squat about weightlifting, please swallow your ego and work with a coach. Self-starter people sometimes make the mistake of thinking they're ready to go it alone pretty early in the learning stages. They've got the kind of temperament that says, "Okay, I've skimmed over the instructions a little. I got this now. Just let me do it myself." This mentality might work when you're assembling a new set of cabinets you bought at Home Depot, but not for weightlifting. If you're in the new or intermediate stages of this business, you need to let somebody else call your shots.

> If you're old and self-reliant and you've got 10-15 years of weightlifting experience, you might not really need to be coached anymore. It all depends on what you're comfortable with. I know some masters athletes who are in their 40s with a long resume in Olympic lifting, but they still want a coach to handle them. They know a ton about the sport, but they just feel better if they're getting guidance. I also know masters lifters who are in their 40s with a long resume in Olympic lifting, and they basically just coach themselves now. I'm like this personally. I've been a competitive athlete for 26 years and a coach for approximately 22 of those years, so I guess I can humbly say that I've got a hefty slice of experience and I know a lot about weightlifting. I don't really need a coach at this point. I know how to train and I definitely know my own limits better than anybody. My technique is very solid and I can film myself to make sure bad habits aren't popping up. You get the point. When you're a grown adult, especially when you've got a strong self-sufficient nature, it might be difficult to put yourself under somebody and take orders, especially if they're younger and less experienced than you. I think

this could make the personality dynamic between the coach and the athlete a little tense. So for those of you who have been banging away in OLifting for a good long while, you might want to ask yourself if a relationship with a coach is a good idea, or something that would even be productive.

Masters weightlifters with no experience: Let's get back to those of you who are starting this thing from ground zero. Actually, you experienced masters need to read this too, because it actually has a lot of application to you.

There aren't many coaches in the sport who specialize in coaching masters weightlifters. We alluded to this in the introduction. The vast majority of the coaches in the world want to train Olympians, National Champions, World Team members, etc. That means they're looking for young athletes. It also means their training mentality is probably going to lean towards much higher volume, frequency, and intensity than an older athlete can handle.

I once knew an older guy who wanted to become a weightlifter and had already talked to a few different coaches about working with him. One of these was a relatively new coach who fancied himself a hardcore taskmaster, so he told this old dude, "My program is hard. If it doesn't break you in half, it'll make you a champion." (I think that was something he heard in a movie or a European coaching lecture). The old guy had a great response. He said, "Listen, I'm 45 years old. I'm not looking to get broken in half. I just want to learn weightlifting."

The point we're making here is that when you're older, it's hard to find a coach who will A) be willing to train you and B) have the required understanding of what it's like to lift weights when you're in the advanced years. Keep in mind, a lot of the coaches in this sport aren't even very old themselves. That means there's no possible way they can truly grasp how your aging body feels. When you're 50 and you've got an ache or a pain, the young coaches will think the same thing they think with their own aches and pains...it'll go away in a couple of days by itself. They've never felt what it's like to be older, when your aches and pains simply don't go away as quickly as they used to.

This means there are certain points that have to be addressed if you're a master lifter and you want to work with a coach:

Experience/teaching: First of all, the coach needs to have a lot of skill in teaching the technique of the OLifts. Obviously this is important for any coach regardless of who they're working with, but it'll be even more important with masters athletes because technical errors can lead to a lot of snap, crackle, and pop in old joints. When youngsters have technique problems, their bodies will have some resilience to the incorrect movements simply because they're young and flexible. You're old and brittle, which means you're going to have a lot more pain when you do things wrong. The coach who's teaching you has to be a stickler for proper movement, and newcomers absolutely have to spend a lot of time working with either an empty bar or extremely light weights to practice the movements. Loading up heavy snatches on a barbell with an old geezer who has bad technique is like jogging through a minefield. It's not gonna take long for something to blow up.

Job/family/life commitments: As if this whole thing wasn't complicated enough, we've also got your real life to think about. If you're a masters athlete, there's a pretty strong chance you've got a job. It's also highly probable that you're married, possibly with children. These things put heavy demands on your time. When you've got commitments like this and you make a decision to pursue Olympic weightlifting, the ugly truth is that the real life stuff will still have to take top priority. Even if you don't want to admit it, your house payment is more important than your workouts. Raising your kids correctly is more important than winning the National Masters Championship.

How does this impact your relationship with your coach? Well, remember what we said about how coaches usually like to focus on working with younger athletes? Young people don't have the life responsibilities I described above, so the coaches can demand complete full-time commitment from them. If the kid misses a workout, the coach can rip the kid's ass because the kid most likely didn't have a good reason for it. That's not how it works with adults. If you're a 48 year-old engineer with a wife and two teenage kids and you're also trying to be a weightlifter, the coach has to understand that he/she can't treat you like you're 17. Because you're old, you're going to take your training seriously. You're not going to miss workouts because you're lazy, or because you want to go to the mall and buy a new skateboard. That's what kids do.

If adults miss workouts, it's probably going to be for a legitimate reason. Skipping a training session so you can attend your daughter's dance recital is a legitimate reason. If you choose your lifting workouts over her recitals, she's might think you don't love her. Then she might grow up to be a stripper. This is why your coach has to understand your life and responsibilities. Being a masters weightlifter and having a coach who's going to chew you out for missing workouts...that's going to be a difficult relationship. The bottom line is that your coach has to be sensible, realistic, and respectful of your life outside the gym.

SAFETY FIRST: You've probably noticed an undertone to this whole book thus far. I'm referring to the constant idea that you'll have to back off the intensity of your training as you get older, and injuries will have to be treated with proper attention. The reason I labeled this concept SAFETY FIRST is because the coach you work with will need to have the appropriate baseline mentality about your training, and I'm talking about the fact that your long-term health and safety is always the top priority. When you're a young athlete, it's okay to push the edge of your physical limits pretty hard because your body is physiologically prepared to handle it. If you're a coach and you work with young kids, you can pound them in training. Their hormones are flowing like a mighty river, and their connective tissue is strong and juicy. You always want to train intelligently and safely, but there's more room with young athletes to go overboard with the intensity...and get away with it. With masters, you won't get away with it as often. Old bodies break easier, so the coach will have to lean towards being careful. I'm not saying that masters athletes shouldn't push their limits. They'll have to push their limits if they want to improve. I'm simply saying that 50 year-old limits are a lot different than 23 year-old limits. Coaches who don't understand this fact can put you in the hospital in the blink of an eye.

Those are some thoughts about coaching. You'll have to examine your life and career, and then make a decision about how/if you want to work with somebody. It's totally dependent on your personal situation, and this section was intended to give you some food for thought. Now that we've covered this issue, we need to steer in a different direction and talk about the teaching/learning process of the Olympic lifts.

Learning Olympic Weightlifting Technique

In the following pages, we're going to outline a very basic learning progression for the Olympic lifts. However, it's important for you to understand that this book is not intended to be a complete training manual for weightlifting. If you're looking for that kind of information, you need to read Greg Everett's book *Olympic Weightlifting: A Complete Guide for Athletes and Coaches.* It covers Olympic weightlifting from A through Z, and it's a great supplement to this book if you're a beginner. Most of the photos you see here are actually taken from it, since Greg is my publisher and he gave permission to use his stuff.

All I want to do in this next section is make sure you've got a solid fundamental perspective on how to learn and perform the basic snatch and clean and jerk. In other words, I'm deliberately not covering every single aspect of the lifts. There are also several technical cues and nuances that I'm not going to mention, for the same reason. So if you've already got familiarity with the OLifts, don't get carried away when you read this and start saying, "Hey! You missed something!" This is just plain vanilla stuff to make sure we're all on the same page, nothing more. We're just giving the OLifts a once-over.

As I've mentioned, some of you might be experienced weightlifters who don't need a beginner's guide to learning the SN and C&J. If that description fits you, you won't need this next section as much as a newbie. If you want to skip ahead, feel free. However, it never hurts to take a fresh look at something you already know. I've looked at the teaching progressions of other coaches and learned some things myself, even with 20+ years of my own experience. If you're an older lifter with OL background, you're probably a coach as well. There might be some strategies in here that you can add to your toolbox.

Learning the Movements: Jump Right In!

When people think about the OLifts for the first time, they're sometimes overwhelmed at how complicated and demanding they are. This often causes people to think they need an extensive time period of "preparation work" before they can start learning the movements. Greg Everett once described this as "people thinking they need a triple-bodyweight front squat before they can start learning the snatch with a PVC pipe."

Here's how you're supposed to look at that, and we'll use a hypothetical example to make it more understandable. Let's say we've got a 41 year-old man named Larry who saw weightlifting on TV at the Olympics and decided he wanted to try the sport himself. Now, Larry doesn't have a background in sports and training. He jogged for a while when he was in his 30s, but that's about it. When Larry comes to a weightlifting gym for his first few workouts, here are the first steps he needs to be put through (after a general warm-up and stretching routine, and I'll outline one of those later). If you bought this book because you're in the same situation as Larry, you can use this next section as your initial guide.

SQUAT

First, Larry has to learn how to **squat**. Personally, I like to take beginners through this progression:

- Bodyweight squat
- Back squat with a stick or PVC pipe
- Back squat with an empty barbell
- Front squat with an empty barbell

PULL

Next, Larry has to learn how to **pull from the floor**. Here's a good progression:

- Learn the starting position of the clean from the floor
- Clean deadlift from mid-shin with a stick or PVC pipe
- Clean deadlift from the floor with a barbell and light training plates, such as 5 lb plastic discs
- Learn the starting position of the snatch from the floor
- Snatch deadlift from the floor with a barbell and light training plates, such as 5 lb plastic discs

Back squat

Front squat

OVERHEAD

Next, Larry has to learn how to **put a barbell over his head**. The progression is:

- BTN (behind-the-neck) military press with a stick or PVC pipe, using a clean-width grip
- BTN (behind-the-neck) military press with a stick or PVC pipe, using a snatch-width grip
- BTN (behind-the-neck) military press with an empty barbell, using a clean-width grip
- BTN (behind-the-neck) military press with an empty barbell, using a snatch-width grip
- Clean-width grip military press from the front of the shoulders with PVC pipe or barbell, depending on the athlete

Clean deadlift

Snatch deadlift

BTN military press with clean grip

BTN military press with snatch grip

These are the bare-bones basics for learning how to lift weights, and there are some important things to remember when using them:

> Don't move forward in the progression until each skill has been learned. In other words, don't start learning step B until step A has been done correctly with consistency.
>
> The speed of the learning progression will depend entirely on the athlete's physical ability. If it takes Larry three weeks to learn how to do the first thing on the checklist (bodyweight squat), then so be it. People with low levels of athletic talent may take a very long time to move through this. People with high levels of athletic talent will go through it in fifteen minutes, and it'll look good.

Military press with clean grip

Once these basics have been mastered, it's time for Larry to start learning the OLifts (snatch, clean and jerk). And let me make something very clear, folks. I'm a huge believer in teaching people step-by-step and being a perfectionist with each one of them. Sloppy mutant technique is not going to be a part of this book. If you want to lift with sloppy mutant technique, put this book down and go buy a different book called *A Complete Guide to Lifting Like a Jackass and Getting Hurt.*

LEARNING THE SNATCH

Overhead Squat

STOP RIGHT THERE! You know...you can learn a lot about somebody when you watch them do their first overhead squat. It's actually a very accurate predictor for how hard the rest of your job is going to be, and we need to spend a minute talking about the important things to look for:

Grip width: I've seen a few different methods for establishing grip width in the snatch. After all the years of teaching the snatch, I've decided that grip width is entirely individual and needs to be established by "eyeballing" from the coach along with feedback from the athlete about what feels stable and comfortable. Almost every CrossFitter I've worked with in recent years uses a snatch grip that's too narrow. The first thing I've had to do with all of them is widen their grip in the bar, and they're usually amazed at how much easier the entire movement feels once they've made the change.

Arm circles

Elbow lockout/overhead flexibility: Some people will immediately be able to stick the bar straight over their ears with locked elbows and a nice wide "spread the wings" chest position. Snatching will be easier for them. Other people will have poor elbow lockout and tight shoulders, making the overhead snatch position awkward and inefficient. Snatching will be difficult for them.

For people with poor flexibility in the overhead snatch position, extra stretching will be mandatory. Here are a few stretches that will be essential for developing the overhead lockout we need:

Bottom position flexibility: If you followed the basic squat progression we listed above, you should have already established squatting proficiency. However, those were back and front squats. Overhead squats change everything for many people because the balance and mobility are much more challenging when the bar is locked out overhead. And this is where we need to cover one of the most important aspects of masters weightlifting: Some

Shoulder dislocates

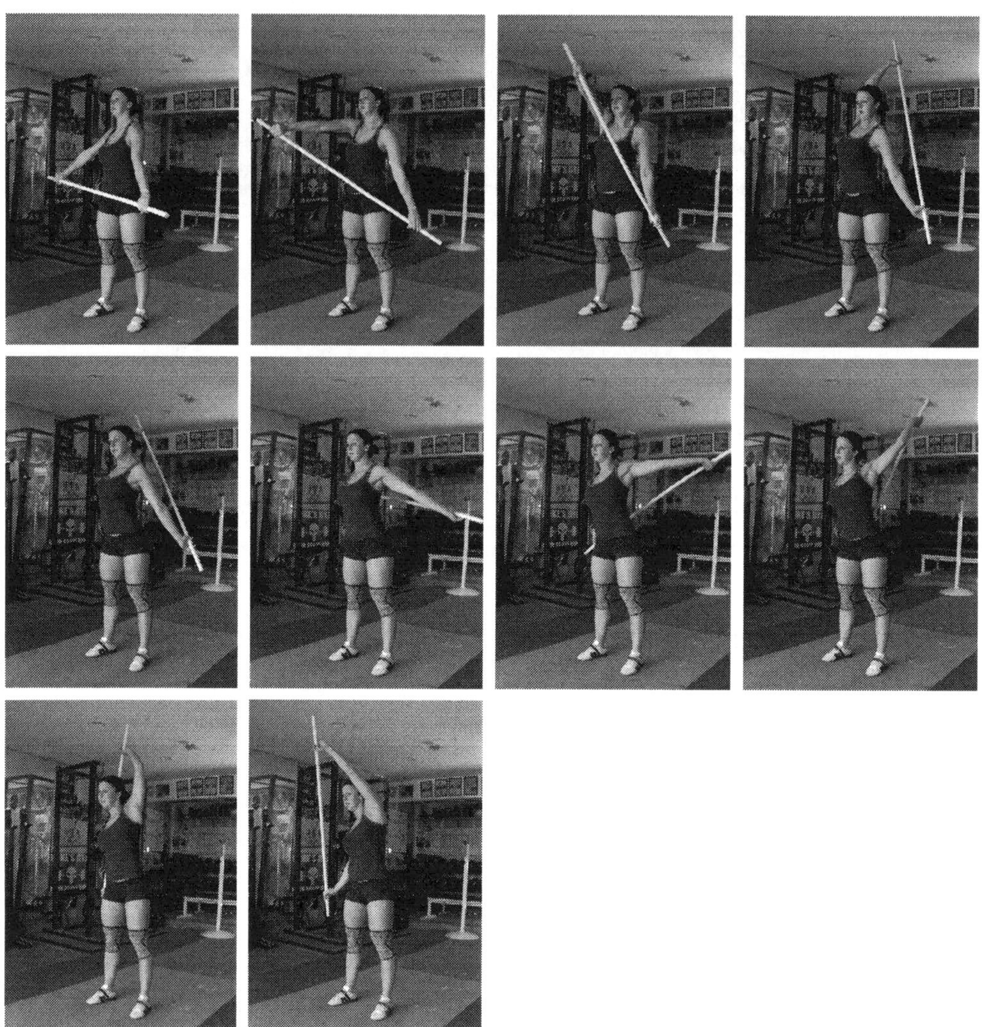

Shoulder pipe rolls

athletes might not be physically capable of sitting down in a full bottom position, at least not at the beginning. If you want to know the hard truth, some people might not EVER be able to sit down in a full bottom position. Athletes who can't sit down in an effective bottom position need to embark on an advanced stretching/mobility program to develop this skill. They'll have to chip away at their flexibility little by little over time, gradually working closer and closer to that deep bottom.

While they're working on their flexibility and progressing down to the bottom position, they should perform power snatches to the lowest bottom point they can effectively hit. In other words, let's say Larry has crappy flexibility and he can only sit down to a half-squat position in the overhead squat.

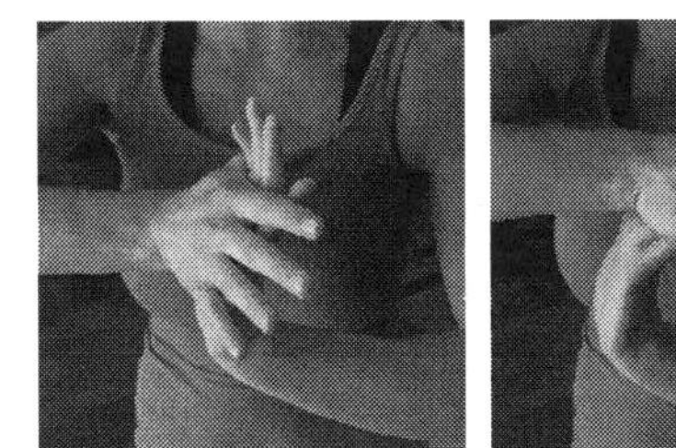
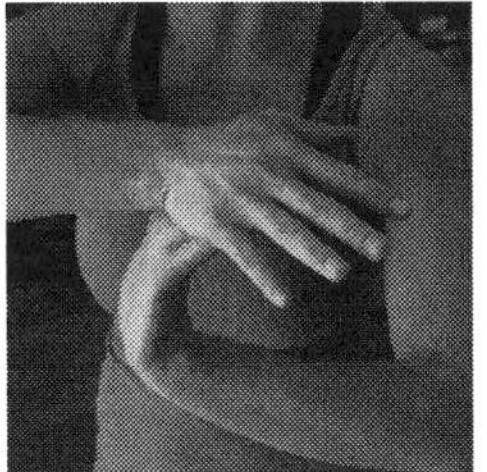
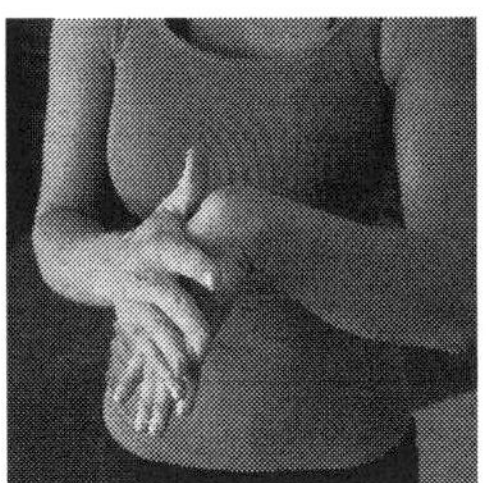
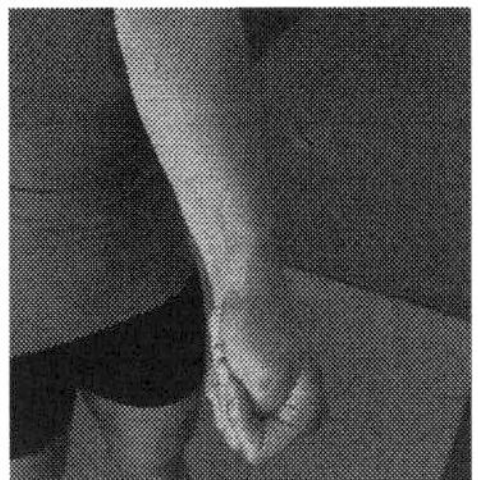

Wrist stretches

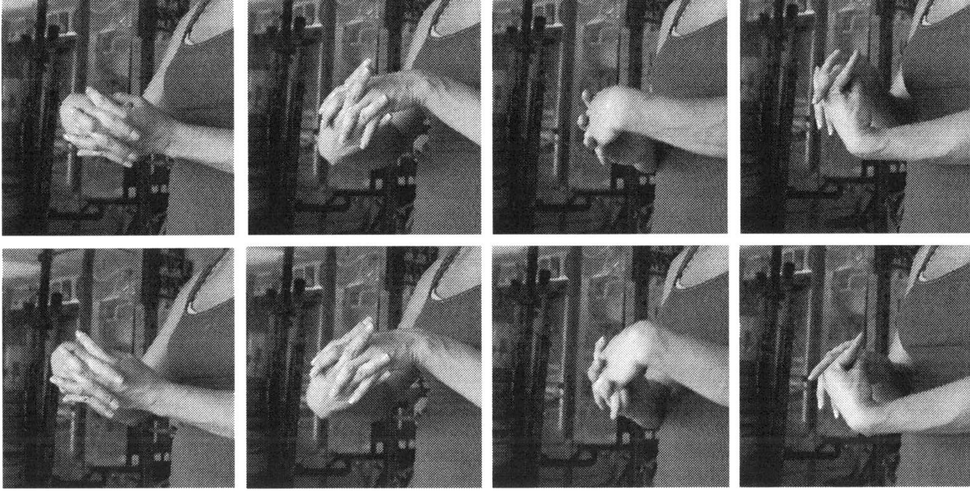

Wrist warm-up

If this is the case, Larry should do power snatches to that half-squat position and practice stable, consistent movement. As his flexibility improves, he'll be able to gradually start taking his power snatches lower and lower. Hopefully, the story will end with Larry being able to do full overhead squats and deep full snatches. But if he's exceptionally tight, it might take a long time to get there. His snatch training becomes twofold:

- Power snatches to the deepest bottom position he can manage
- Daily flexibility work before and after snatching to improve his depth and range of motion

How long will it take to learn full overhead squats and snatches? That totally depends on the athlete. Is this a perfect world? NO. But look at it this way...you're old. Nothing is going to be perfect anymore, so you'll just have to improvise, adapt, and overcome.

Pulling Stance

As with grip width, this is highly individual. A cue I like to use is telling the athlete to put their feet where they would be for a standing vertical jump. I tell them to imagine they're standing under a basketball hoop, preparing to jump up and touch the rim. Where would they put their feet for that? This usually gets them in the right ballpark for foot width, although I often have to move them closer by just a smidge from the vertical jump placement. I also prefer to have the toes pointing straight forward, although some athletes might need to have the toes pointed slightly out if they're bowlegged. Once foot width has been established, the athlete can be moved to learning the actual pulling movements.

Hook Grip

The fingers wrap around the thumb when the athlete grips the barbell. This is standard for all Olympic lifts that involve some kind of pulling movement (not for jerks or squats).

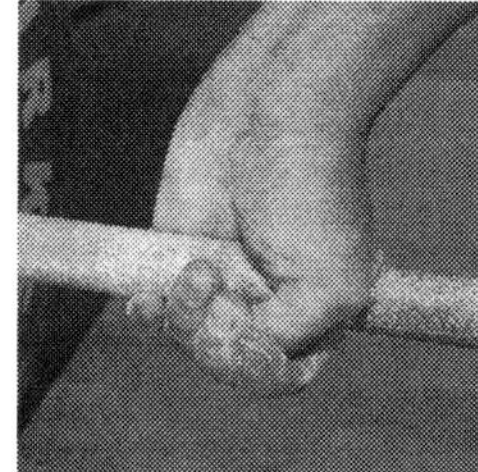

The hook grip

Power Snatch from the Hips

The athlete will let the bar hang down at arm's length. From there, the following cues should be taught:

- Back flat
- Shoulder blades pinched together, "standing up straight" posture, chest out
- Elbows turned out (toward the sides)
- Knuckles down
- Eyes straight ahead
- Bend the knees around six inches or so, where the bar is tucked into the hip joint
- Feet flat on the floor, bodyweight in the middle of the foot
- Back still straight up and down, no forward lean

This is the start position for this movement. Once this position is solidified, the pulling mechanics can be taught following this sequence:

Power snatch from the hips

- First, have the athlete extend tall onto the toes and shrug the shoulders, arms still straight. Practice multiple reps of this.
- Next, have the athlete jump and shrug. The athlete will actually jump a few inches into the air while simultaneously shrugging the shoulders, arms still straight.
- Stand with feet and legs motionless and teach the movement of the arms. This is what happens when the shrug has been completed and the arms pull upward as the turnover starts (when the athlete jumps down into the bottom position). The elbows pull upwards toward the ceiling and the bar stays close to the abdomen and chest. The shrug happens first: shrug-arms, shrug-arms, etc.
- Once these movements have been repped, the athlete is ready to perform a power snatch from the hips. (This is the point where they will need to be taught about jumping their feet from pulling width to squat width. You might want to practice this a few times without the snatch movement, simply have the athlete hop the feet from the pull width position to their overhead squat position.)

Multiple reps of this movement should be performed until the lift looks consistent and correct. Once again, the athlete should not move on to the next step until this one has been mastered.

Snatch from the Hips

All of the cues from the previous movement should be continually reinforced, but now the athlete will simply transition into a full squat snatch movement instead of a power snatch. This will likely take several reps and a lot of time to master. Even if the athlete picks up the movement quickly, multiple reps (sets of five) should still be performed.

Hang Power Snatch above the Knee

All of the cues from the previous movement should be continually reinforced, but now the athlete lowers the bar to directly above the kneecap for the start position.

- The knees will be bent and the torso will be angled forward. Looking at the athlete directly from the side, the shoulders should be over the bar.
- The athlete should practice transitioning from the kneecap position back to the hips (starting position of the previous movement). This will begin the athlete on the process of learning the double-knee bend, which is often the most complicated part of learning the OLifts.
- Once this transition movement (moving the bar from the kneecap to the hips) has been practiced, the power snatch from hang above the knee can be practiced.

Above the knee hang position

NOTE: *When taking an athlete through this learning progression, I prefer to have them do at least three or four sets of five reps with an empty barbell (or light training bar if their strength level is low). You can't go wrong with a lot of movement-learning reps.*

Hang Snatch above the Knee

All of the cues from the previous movement should be continually reinforced, but now the athlete will simply transition into a full squat snatch movement instead of a power snatch. This will likely take several reps and a lot of time to master. Even if the athlete picks up the movement quickly, multiple reps (sets of five reps) should still be performed.

Starting Position

When learning the start position from the floor, the athlete can do one of two things:

- Lower the bar to the middle of the shin.
- Put 2.5 or 5 lb plastic training plates on the bar and simply set it on the platform. I prefer this method. Big strong guys can probably use a 10 lb training plate.

The following cues should be taught:

- The bar should be in contact with the shins.
- Back tight, arms straight, elbows out, knuckles down... the same cues are reinforced throughout the entire teaching progression.
- The hips will be slightly elevated, enough to put the shoulders directly above the bar when observing the athlete from the side
- The athlete should be taught to hold this position for 5-10 seconds at a time, just to memorize it.
- Once the start position has been mastered, the athlete is ready to do a power snatch from the floor.

Snatch starting position

Power snatch

Power Snatch

All of the same cues from the previous steps need to be reinforced. Don't emphasize speed too much in the beginning, but don't require the athlete to move slowly either. Worry about whether they're hitting the right positions, keeping the bar close to the body, and practicing all the technical points that have already been worked on throughout the teaching progression.

Snatch

All of the cues from the previous movement should be continually reinforced, but now the athlete will simply transition into a full squat snatch movement instead of a power snatch. This will likely take several reps and a lot of time to master. Even if the athlete picks up the movement quickly, multiple reps (sets of five reps) should still be performed.

Snatch

At this point, the athlete has learned how to snatch. It won't look perfect, but hopefully it won't look horrible either. Once the athlete can perform effective full snatches, I prefer to drop power snatches and spend most of the practice time on the full movements. The only way they're really going to learn a full movement is to practice it over and over and over. Power snatches, in my opinion, are distracting to beginners. They'll often revert back to power snatches when they get into trouble, and I like to remove that option from the equation. I know some coaches have different methods, and that's fine. My method is basically just my own preference based on practice as an athlete and a coach. In fact, it's important to know that this learning progression is simply the one I personally like to use when teaching these movements. Other coaches have variations on how they like to teach, so my method isn't a universal law. There are many effective progressions that will lead an athlete to the proper movements. This is one of them, but it's not the only one.

LEARNING THE CLEAN

I use almost the exact same teaching progression for the snatch and the clean. Therefore, much of this information is basically a repeat of what you read above, with the appropriate adjustments for the different elements of the movement.

Front Squat

As with the overhead squat, this position can be a very challenging one for masters athletes. Old people are often stiff and inflexible, and it's obvious from looking at the photo that flexibility is in high demand with the front squat position. If you're lucky enough to be one of those athletes who has an easy time hitting this front squat position and sitting down there like you were born to do it, you've got a huge gift that you aren't even aware of. In order to make sure the athlete is in the best possible position to execute this skill, the following points need to be addressed:

Behind the neck barbell stretch

Grip width: The grip in the front squat is easy to figure out because it's the same as the clean deadlift from the floor that the athlete should have already practiced. Generally, the athlete is going to want to grab the bar in a position where their hands are just slightly outside their shoulders. They need to have their hands close enough to get their elbows up nice and high, but not so close that their shoulders are bunched up and uncomfortable. The length of the athlete's arms, along with the mobility they have in their wrists, elbows, and shoulders will determine how easy it is to hold this position. As with the overhead position in the snatch, grip width is highly

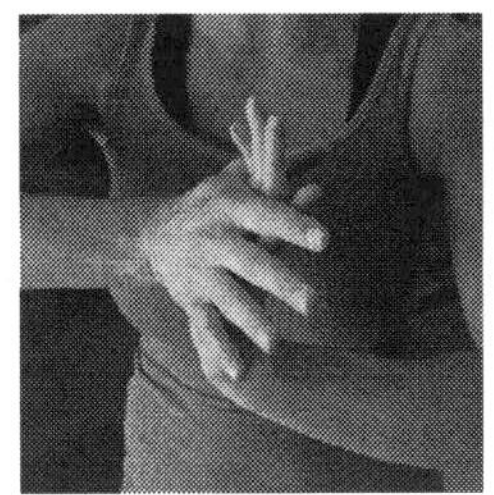
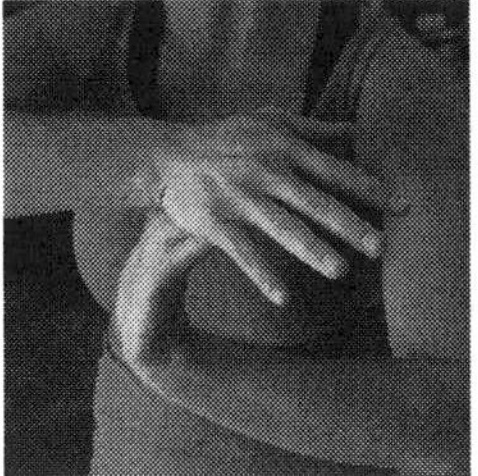
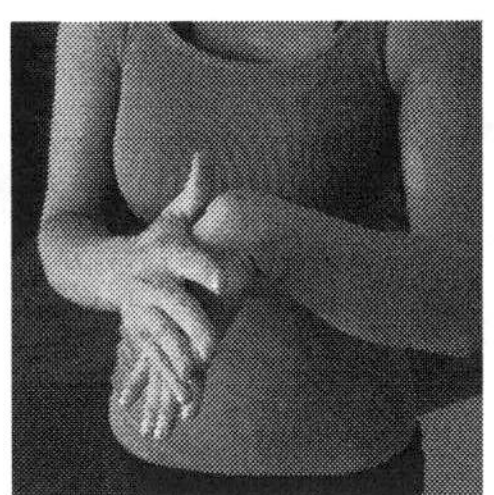
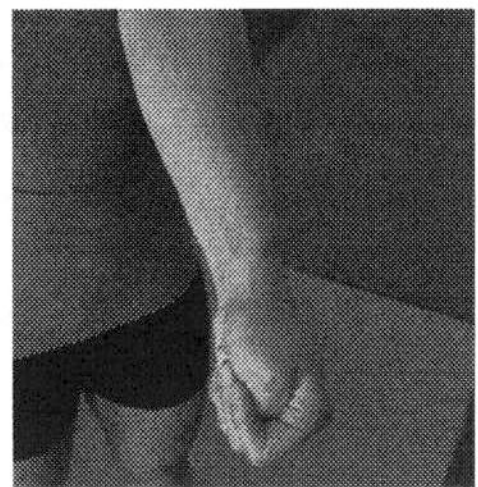

Wrist stretches

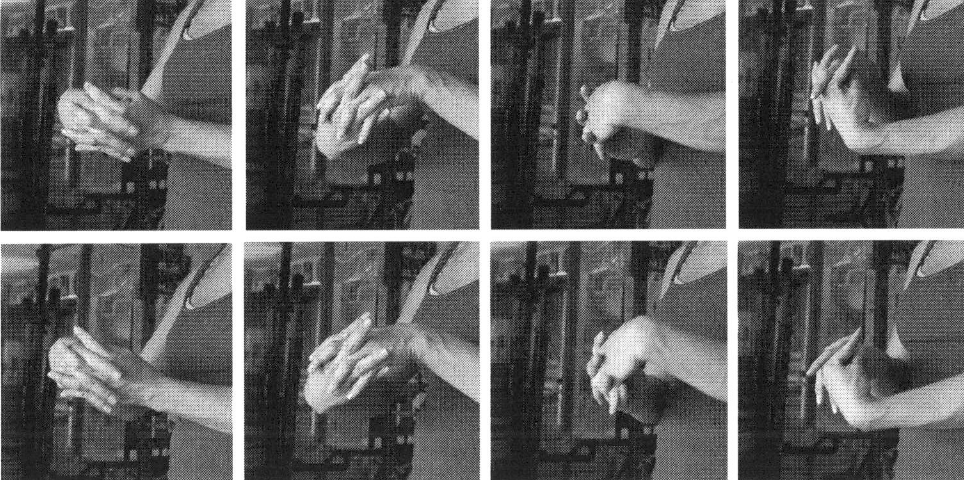

Wrist warm-up

individual and you might need to play around with some adjustments before you settle on a permanent one.

For people with poor flexibility in the front squat position, extra stretching will be mandatory. Here are a few stretches that will be essential for developing the flexibility we need.

Partner-assisted rack stretch

Bottom position flexibility: As with the snatch, we need to remember the following rules. Some of this is intentionally repeated word-for-word from the previous snatch section, because I really want to hammer this point home: Some athletes might not be physically capable of sitting down in a full bottom position, at least not at the beginning. If you want to know the hard

Front squat

truth, some people might not EVER be able to sit down in a full bottom position. Athletes who can't sit down in an effective bottom position need to embark on an advanced stretching/mobility program to develop this skill. They'll have to chip away at their flexibility little by little over time, gradually working closer and closer to that deep bottom.

While they are working on their flexibility and progressing down to the bottom position, they should perform power cleans to the lowest bottom point they can effectively hit. In other words, let's say Larry has crappy flexibility and he can only sit down to a half-squat position in the front squat. If this is the case, Larry should do power cleans to that half-squat position and practice stable, consistent movement. As his flexibility improves, he'll be able to gradually start taking his power cleans lower and lower. Hopefully, the story will end with Larry being able to do full front squats and deep full cleans. But if he's exceptionally tight, it might take a long time to get there. His clean training becomes twofold:

- Power cleans to the deepest bottom position he can manage
- Daily flexibility work before and after snatching to improve his depth and range of motion

How long will it take to learn full front squats and cleans? That totally depends on the athlete. Is this a perfect world? NO. But look at it this way... you're old. Nothing is going to be perfect anymore, so you'll just have to improvise, adapt, and overcome.

Pulling Stance

This should be done in the same manner as the snatch.

Hook Grip

Remind them that hook gripping is non-negotiable for Olympic lifters. You have to do it, period.

Power Clean from the Hips

The athlete will let the bar hang down at arm's length. From there, the following cues should be taught:

- Back flat
- Shoulder blades pinched together, "standing up straight" posture, chest out
- Elbows turned out (toward the sides)
- Knuckles down
- Eyes straight ahead
- Bend the knees around six inches or so; the bar will obviously be at a lower point on the thigh than in the snatch because of the narrower hand spacing. This is a normal part of the lift. *(NOTE: Because of the fact that the bar will not be tucked into the hip joint in the clean, as it is in the snatch, referring to this drill as "Power clean from the hips" may sound misleading. Here's the reasoning behind it: even though the bar position on the thighs/hips is different between the two movements, I still like to describe them both as "from the hips" simply because it keeps the teaching progression more uniform and easier for athletes to remember. Once they've had this point explained, the "from the hips" phrase shouldn't be confusing. I've done it this way with athletes throughout my whole coaching career, and it's never a problem as long as they understand this difference.)*
- Feet flat on the floor, bodyweight in the middle of the foot
- Back still straight up and down, no forward lean
- This is the start position for this movement. Once this position is solidified, the pulling mechanics can be taught following this sequence:

    - First, have the athlete extend tall onto the toes and shrug the shoulders, arms still straight. Practice multiple reps of this.

Power clean from the hips

- Next, have the athlete jump and shrug: The athlete will actually jump a few inches into the air while simultaneously shrugging the shoulders, arms still straight.
- Stand with feet and legs motionless and teach the movement of the arms. This is what happens when the shrug has been completed and the arms pull upward as the turnover starts (when the athlete jumps down into the bottom position). The elbows pull upwards toward the ceiling and the bar stays close to the abdomen and chest. The shrug happens first: shrug-arms, shrug-arms, etc.
- Once these movements have been repped, the athlete is ready to perform a power clean from the hips. This is the point where they will need to be taught about jumping their feet from pulling width to squat width. You might want to practice this a few times without the snatch movement, simply have the athlete hop the feet from the pull width position to their front squat position.

Multiple reps of this movement should be performed, until the lift looks consistent and correct. Once again, the athlete should not move on to the next step until this one has been mastered.

Clean from the Hips

All of the cues from the previous movement should be continually reinforced, but now the athlete will simply transition into a full squat clean movement instead of a power clean. This will likely take several reps and a lot of time to master. Even if the athlete picks up the movement quickly, multiple reps (sets of five reps) should still be performed.

Hang Power Clean from above the Knee

All of the cues from the previous movement should be continually reinforced, but now the athlete lowers the bar to directly above the kneecap for the start position.

- The knees will be bent and the torso will be angled forward. Looking at the athlete directly from the side, the shoulders should be over the bar.
- Again, the athlete should practice transitioning from the kneecap position back to the mid/upper thigh (starting position of the previous movement). This will continue the process of learning the double-knee bend.
- Once this transition movement (moving the bar from the kneecap to the mid/upper thigh) has been practiced, the power snatch from hang above the knee can be practiced.

Above the knee hang position

NOTE: When taking an athlete through this learning progression, I prefer to have them do at least three or four sets of five reps with an empty barbell (or light training bar if their strength level is low). You can't go wrong with a lot of movement-learning reps.

Hang Clean from above the Knee

All of the cues from the previous movement should be continually reinforced, but now the athlete will simply transition into a full squat clean movement instead of a power clean. This will likely take several reps and a lot of time to master. Even if the athlete picks up the movement quickly, multiple reps (sets of five reps) should still be performed.

Starting Position

As with the snatch, when learning the start position from the floor, the athlete can do one of two things:

- Lower the bar to the middle of the shin.
- Put 2.5 or 5 lb plastic training plates on the bar and simply set it on the platform. I prefer this method. Big strong guys can probably use a 10 lb training plate.

The following cues should be reinforced:

Clean starting position

- The bar should be in contact with the shins.
- Back tight, arms straight, elbows out, knuckles down... the same cues are reinforced throughout the entire teaching progression.
- The hips will be slightly elevated, enough to put the shoulders directly above the bar when observing the athlete from the side
- The athlete should be taught to hold this position for 5-10 seconds at a time, just to memorize it.
- Once the start position has been mastered, the athlete is ready to do a power clean from the floor.

Power clean

Power Clean

All of the same cues from the previous steps need to be reinforced. Don't emphasize speed too much in the beginning, but don't require the athlete to move slowly either. Worry about whether they're hitting the right positions, keeping the bar close to the body, and practicing all the technical points that have already been worked on throughout the teaching progression.

Clean

All of the cues from the previous movement should be continually reinforced, but now the athlete will simply transition into a full squat clean movement instead of a power clean. This will likely take several reps and a lot of time to master. Even if the athlete picks up the movement quickly, multiple reps (sets of five reps) should still be performed.

Clean

LEARNING THE JERK

BTN (behind-the-neck) Military Press

ress from behind the neck with a stick or PVC pipe, using a clean-width grip (this is the same movement from the initial learning progression we did with Larry).

Clean-grip Military Press

Press from the front of the shoulders with PVC pipe or barbell, depending on the athlete (once again, the same movement we did with Larry).

Jerk Dip

Here, the athlete needs to practice the initial dip phase of the jerk, using the following cues:

- The bar sits on the shoulders, like a completed clean.
- The feet should be in a position fairly close to where they are at the beginning of the pull. Some athletes like a slightly wider stance than this.
- The elbows may be lowered slightly from where they were when the clean was being completed. A position like this is effective for the jerk. However, when lowering the elbows slightly, it's essential to do the following:
  - Maintain upright posture with the upper body throughout the dip
  - Don't allow the shoulders to droop forward
  - Don't allow the upper back to round forward
  - Tight, solid abdomen and core
- The athlete should bend the knees around 5-6 inches. The exact depth of the dip should be determined by eyeballing from the coach. I usually say 5-6 inches simply because almost everybody goes too shallow when they first start practicing the dip.
- The athlete should think *dip through the heels*. I use the cue "drop your butt between your heels when you dip" to avoid shifting forward onto the toes, which is a big no-no.
- I like to have athletes practice the dip only before moving on to the next movement.

Jerk rack position

Push press

Push Press

Here, the athlete dips, then drives upwards with the legs. The leg extension flows directly into the press over the head. These cues are important:

- Leg drive is first, arm extension is last.
- The bar (or stick) should be locked out over the ears with the eyes facing forward.
- The feet don't come off the ground in this movement. They can extend up on the toes during the top of the drive phase, but no separation from the ground should occur.

Push Jerk

In this movement, the athlete follows the exact same cues from the push press. But at the finish of this movement, the feet are going to drive off the

Push jerk

ground and jump slightly out to the sides (much like the movement of catching a power clean or snatch). The athlete will lock the bar out overhead while simultaneously jumping down slightly into a shallow squat position. (Some people call this a power jerk, which is fine because they're the same movement with interchangeable names. But a push/power jerk is not the same as a squat jerk. That's something entirely different.)

Split Position

Let me walk you through how I do this:

- Stand behind the athlete and push them forward. Whichever foot they step forward with to steady themselves is the foot they need to put forward on the split.
- Have the athlete step forward with that foot, while reaching the other foot back behind them.

Split position

- Have them position the front leg so the shin is straight up and down. The toe should be straight, or turned slightly inward.
- Have them position the back foot so that the heel is off the ground and the toe is straight.
- Have them bend the back knee to a point that brings their hips directly under their shoulders and also looks balanced and stable.
- Tell them to check their position to make sure they have even weight distribution between the front and back foot.
- The split position is highly individual, so the coach basically needs to work with the athlete until they're in a position that closely resembles this

Split Footwork

Multiple reps of dipping and driving, like the push jerk, while punching the legs into the split position and holding it for a second or two to establish balance. The athletes should use a two-step recovery, with the front foot always recovering first, then the back foot, until they are standing with both feet even.

Split Jerk

This is the big Kahuna. If the athletes have mastered the previous steps in the process, the split jerk should happen fairly easily. Some people will have trouble with it, which is normal. Athletes should practice with an empty bar until the movement is stable, consistent, and balanced.

NOTE: Any of these movements can be performed from behind the neck (BTN). This can be a useful tool if the athlete is having difficulty locking the bar out in the correct position overhead. Some coaches like to use them as

Split jerk

part of their teaching progression full-time, simply because they like the value. I've done it both ways over the years.

Summation

That's enough for now. As I said, this is simply one quick example of how you can teach the Olympic lifts to beginners. I've used several different teaching methods over the years, including this one. I understand many of you aren't beginners, and you might be way past the progression we just reviewed. But I'm also aware there's a population of people who might be reading this book because they saw weightlifting on TV during the Olympics and they decided to give it a try at 48 years old. Those people need to be moved along step-by-step, which is the reason for this section. There's a wide range of assistance exercises, other technical cues, pointers, and general pieces of input that could be added to what I gave you. There are other books that teach these things, and many of them are available through Catalyst Athletics. You should continue to explore those things throughout your weightlifting career by reading, watching, talking, and practicing. This was your basic introduction, and you should feel free to use it when you teach the OLifts to others. I've been using this exact progression for a while now, and it works.

SECTION FOUR

Programming and Training

At this point, we've developed the proper mindset for embarking on your masters OLifting journey, and we've learned how to perform the lifts. These are two of the most important bricks in the foundation of this whole thing, but they're also very basic preliminary steps. For some of you who are more experienced than a bare-bones beginner, much of the stuff we've looked at is like review material. You veterans have already been banging it out in this sport for a long time, so you've got the mental perspective covered. And if you've got prior experience, you might have been able to skip ahead past the last section because you've been snatching and clean & jerking for years and you don't need to follow a basic learning progression. For those of you who fit this description, don't worry. I already know what you were hoping to get from this book when you decided to read it. You wanted suggestions and ideas for how to develop a more effective training program.

Aaahhh, now we're talking. Listen, this upcoming section is one of the main reasons I decided to write this thing. As we mentioned in the very beginning, there isn't a lot of training information available for old weightlifters. I actually just got a message on Facebook yesterday from a woman who competes in the 50-54 age division, and she was complaining about how the internet, with its vast ocean of resources, is practically bone dry when it comes to masters weightlifting programs. You can find plenty of programming information that might work wonders if you're in your teens or twenties. That stuff isn't hard to locate. But looking for reliable, useful training ideas that are specifically designed for aging lifters? That's a horse of a different color. There just isn't much of it out there, brothers and sisters.

In this section, you're going to get a great deal of training information that comes straight from highly successful masters weightlifters who were kind enough to share their ideas with me. I wanted to make sure we provided a wide range of input in this book from people who have actually figured out a way to extend their lifting careers into the grey-hair stage without landing on a surgeon's table every eight months. Fortunately, I found a lot of good guys and gals who were willing to chip in for your benefit.

However, there's something very important we need to do before the nuts-and-bolts info gets delivered. We need to review some basic rules. These rules apply to all of you, whether you like it or not. These are like the Ten Commandments, or the Five Pillars of Islam, something in that range. In fact, let's give them a cool name just to jazz things up...

The Three Cornerstones of Geezer Weightlifting

1. Thou shalt be forced to train differently when you're older

Seriously, I just can't believe how many people never seem to figure this out. To my way of thinking, this one is so elementary and obvious that I almost hesitate to write about it. It's the weightlifting version of common sense. But there are a lot of people out there (and I know I'm stepping on some toes with this) who just won't accept the facts. Here's what I mean:

- When you are young, your body is in a certain condition and it's capable of certain things.
- When you are old, your body is in a different condition and it's no longer capable of the same things.
- Because this is true, you have to train differently when you're old. You have no choice.

And despite how clear and indisputable those concepts are, the OLifting graveyard is still littered with casualties who could have had exciting masters careers if they just would have accepted the truth. Instead of acceptance, they made a decision to live like superhuman terminators of power, and they kept training in their 30s and 40s the same way they used to in their 20s. Actually, I should correct that sentence. They TRIED to keep training in their 30s and 40s the same way they used to in their 20s, and their bodies went kaplooey. Injuries forced them out of the sport, and it was their own damn fault.

I think this mindset comes partially from all the hyper-inspirational media advertising we get bombarded with on a daily basis. We see these NOTHING IS IMPOSSIBLE advertising slogans from Nike or Reebok or whoever, accompanied by a photo of a leper with no hands paddling a kayak down a raging river. Commercials come on TV with dramatic piano music playing in the background where we see a 20-second documentary of somebody who got hit by a train and diagnosed with eight types of cancer, and then went on to win the New York Marathon. You feel like a lazy turd compared to these people. In other words, the world we live in today tries to convince all of us that we can overcome any obstacle. They want us to believe the rules of normal limitations don't apply to us. And by the way, you need to buy the new Jordans to accomplish these things.

This stuff is awesome, admittedly. Little bits of motivation are great fuel for our lives, and I'm not dissing them. Hell, some of you might have decided to try masters weightlifting because of how excited you got from watching that leper in the kayak. In that case... excellent!

However, the flip side of this phenomenon is that many people reject the idea that they have any limits at all. That can get you into scary territory. You see, there's a sensitive balance between courage and stupidity. Being a competitive athlete in your older years is courageous. Refusing to accept the facts of basic biology is stupid. I really, really hope you understand this. I might sound like I'm overdoing the world's most obvious facts, but I realize some of you are hard chargers who don't want to back off. You're stubborn, which is a good thing. But it can get you in some trouble if you don't blend it with intelligence.

Age WILL put limitations on you. It won't limit your spirit or your determination, but it will limit the amount of strength and power your muscles can generate. It will limit your ability to recover quickly from hard workouts. It will limit the elasticity of your tendons and ligaments. And because of this, you simply have to smarten up and concede, at some point, that you'll have to train differently as your birthdays pile up. Ignore this rule at thy peril.

2. Thou shalt be forced to back off when you're older

Obviously this is a continuation of cornerstone #1. We first establish that you're going to have to do things differently when you're older. From there, we establish that "doing things differently" means you're going to have to do LESS. It's kind of like the Ten Commandments in the Bible, where they tell you not to commit adultery...and then later they tell you not to covet your neighbor's wife. You get ten rules for living your life, and two of them are about sexual indiscretions. Likewise, the Three Cornerstones of Geezer Weightlifting have some overlap too. #1 basically bleeds into #2.

Backing off, brothers and sisters. That's all we're talking about here. If you want to make it through the long haul in OLifting, you'll have to learn to pull back on a lot of things. Volume, intensity, frequency...all of it. And as we mentioned already, this is a challenge to your pride and enthusiasm.

When you're older, your athletic life means a lot more to you than it does when you're young. You understand that you're very lucky to even still be healthy enough to lift weights in your old age. You treasure your training because it's one of the best parts of your day. The thought of losing it scares the crap out of you. Because it means so much, you want to enjoy it to the fullest. That means you want to train hard and often.

You won't make it as a masters weightlifter if you don't find a way to pull back on how hard and often you train. You could train hard six days a week when you were a kid? Gotcha. You might have to train moderately two or three days a week when you're old. You don't believe me? Fine, keep going full blast and see how long you last. You probably won't break down right away, but it'll happen eventually. As sure as God made little red apples, you'll break down. When you're young, it takes a lot of self-discipline to train hard all the time. When you're old, it takes a lot of self-discipline to stay OUT of the gym when you need to.

3. Thou shalt be forced to pay more attention to nutrition and taking care of your body when you're older

Can you believe some of the things you got away with when you were a kid? Did any of you party a lot when you were young, maybe in your college years or whatever? Remember when you could hit the bar until 2 am, get hammered drunk off your ass, crawl home and get four hours of sleep...and then train like a maniac the next day? Does that ring a bell?

I know some of you might come from very strict backgrounds where you didn't really have any wild days. If you're a Mormon, the wild phase of your life might have been the years when you stayed out until 11:30 pm, drank caffeinated soda, and skipped family home evening once a month. If that's your story, it's cool.

But for those of you (like me) who went full-tilt boogie back in the day, isn't it crazy to think how resilient your body was back then? You could defile yourself in a variety of creative ways, and you would still be feeling great and ready to rock by noon the next day. And that's just talking about drinking and lack of sleep. We haven't even looked at nutrition yet.

Remember when you could eat anything you wanted, with almost no consequences? I'm talking about the days when your dinner could be a box of greasy tacos and burritos from Taco Bell, with some chocolate Ding Dongs for dessert, and it wouldn't change anything about you. You wouldn't get fat and flabby, and your stomach could digest that garbage without a hitch. Now it's different, right? When you're old, try going out and stringing together a bunch of Taco Bell and Ding Dong dinners. You spend the rest of the night having a turbulent relationship with your toilet, and the extra fat and sugar hits your ass like a cottage cheese cannonball.

Things hurt a lot more when you're old too. Now we understand why our dads grunted like rhinos when they got up from their recliners. Their bodies were achy, and now yours is too. It wasn't like that when you were a kid. If you got hurt, it only lasted for a short time. If you had an injury, it went away pretty quickly unless it was a broken bone or something like that. Now, injuries stick around for a nice long visit. A muscle pull that would have been gone in three days when you were 22 will bug you for three weeks when you're 50.

You can't get away from this. And if it makes you feel any better, you can't get away from it even if you don't lift weights. As we've mentioned, most of the decrepit old farts limping around the world didn't get that way from hard training. They got that way from doing nothing. So if you're going to be in pain anyway, you might as well get strong and have some big muscles along the way. However, you'll have to clean things up if you want to make your weightlifting last. Diet, hydration, injury prevention, taking care of your body... those things will have to become a much bigger part of your life. If you address them intelligently, you'll probably feel a lot better. We'll cover them later, after we talk about what you need to do with the barbell.

Programming Phase One: Proper Warm-up and Preparation

Now we actually start to explore your workouts and weekly training programs. We're going to analyze this systematically, meaning we'll start at the beginning. Before we even look at the lifting you're going to do, we need to talk about warming up.

One of the underlying ideas in this book so far is that your body will be more stiff and achy as you get older. That means you'll have to use a very effective daily warm-up before you even touch the barbell because your joints and muscles will have to be primed and ready when you jump under that first snatch. As we mentioned in the Three Cornerstones, this is another area where you could get away with a lot of negligence when you were young. Back then, you could probably charge in and start your workouts with a bare minimum of warm-up and preparation. Now, it's different. You HAVE to put some effort into a daily warm-up, so let me walk you through the best way to do it.

Actually, I'm going to do this by giving you something I've already published. The following is an excerpt from an article I wrote in the Catalyst Athletics online magazine *Performance Menu* in 2013. In the months after this article was released, I received quite a few positive comments from lifters who said they had started implementing this warm-up information into their own training. A few of the lifters I'm currently coaching are still using it before each training session. It got great reviews, so I like the idea of delivering it to you as part of this book. Here it is:

- -

Reduce Your Pain Level...100% Guaranteed

Excerpt from Performance Menu Issue 96 - January 2013

Okay, I want you to visualize a situation with me. You'll need to see and feel the things I'm going to describe.

You're in the gym and you're getting ready to start a workout. You've just finished putting your shoes on and it's time to start warming up. Now, this is during a time period when you've been training really hard. You've been hitting a lot of maximum attempts in the snatch and clean & jerk, along with pushing your squats and pulls about as heavy as you've ever gone. Training has been good, but you've paid the price. What I mean by that is you're living with some pain right now. And so you're sitting on the bench with your shoes on, getting ready for your workout, and you sit there for just a couple of seconds and realize something in your head: "Okay, this is gonna hurt."

You're not injured right now, mind you. You don't have any tears or pulls that are going to force you to change your workouts. You're just hurting, that's all. You've got what we call "training pain" and you're thinking about how your wrists, knees, back, shoulders and elbows are going to feel when you put your hands on the bar and perform your first snatches of the day. It's not pleasant. But you're not a wimp, so you step up to the platform and get started anyway. The people in your gym can see the little scrunching-up facial gestures you make when you put that bar over your head the first few times and then sit down in the bottom position. They get it, because they're hurting too.

I want to look at some effective ways to prepare your body before you even touch the barbell. These are things that can drastically reduce how bad your joints feel when you start your lifts, so you should keep reading if you want things to hurt less.

When you were young, you could just walk in the gym, loosen up for two minutes, hit the barbell as hard as possible with some max attempts, and then walk out and go home. Your body was producing hormones so fast that your recovery time was almost instantaneous. You didn't live with huge levels of pain. Some soreness, sure. But not the kind of stuff we were just talking about. Well, most of you who are reading this aren't young anymore. So if you want to keep training and making progress, you damn well better be interested in finding some warm-up and restorative methods that will make your training experience easier and more effective.

I'm trying to help you hurt less, brothers and sisters. Unless you're a masochist, you should WANT to hurt less. Fortunately for you, I've been training for many years and I'm getting older now, and I've managed to find a few surefire tactics that keep me from living in a world of agony. Now, I'm passing them on to you.

Warm-Up, Chinese-Style…

Anybody with some serious training experience has felt the sting of starting your first few sets before your body is primed and ready to lift. Your joints are tight, you can't get yourself into the right positions, and you're getting some pretty big pain from some pretty small weights. It sucks, big time. We often wind up devoting a ton of time to warm-up/stretching preparation.

I've heard a few older lifters make the joke, "It takes an hour to warm up and thirty minutes to lift." What I'm going to do here is simple. I'm just going to give you my exact warm-up routine (what I do before I put weights on the bar and start lifting). This is what I've been doing to get ready for my workouts for the last five or six years, and I can't say enough about how happy I've been with it. I've tried a lot of different warm-up methods in the past, and there is no doubt that this one is the best progression I've ever used.

I've learned some of this from different lifters and coaches over the years, but most of it comes from the videos I've seen from the Chinese weightlifting program. They've got extensive warm-up progressions they go through, together as a team, before they start their workouts. These videos are on YouTube, and I've also trained with some people who have been to China and verified how their lifters do it. I hate to glorify the Chinese so much because I'm a patriotic American, but dammit...they've got things figured out, don't they? Their success is a result of their efficient methods (along with a lot of other things), so my ears are always open when I hear somebody say, "In China, the lifters and coaches..." So, this is what I do before I lift:

- 10-15 standing hops: This is as simple as it sounds, I just stand there and hop up in the air ten or fifteen times, not trying for maximum height and not pausing between hops. Just up and down like a pogo stick, getting maybe four or five inches off the ground, great way to get the ankles and knees ready for a little ballistic impact.
- 10-15 jumping jacks: Now I'm activating the groin and the muscles of the upper body, still getting good ballistic movement.
- 10-15 standing hops: Back to the hops again.
- 10-15 high knee/butt kicks: These are just basic track and field warm-up exercises, high knee jogging in place, alternating with butt kickers, now we're starting to get the hamstrings, quads, and glutes loose.
- All of these first four exercises are done consecutively with no pause between—one just runs right into the next one.
- 15 horizontal arm swings: Now I'm just standing still, swinging the arms back and forth across my chest, trying to keep them long and get them as far behind me as possible on the backswing.

- 15 arm circles: Windmill-type circles, one arm at a time, 15 circles with each arm, keeping the arms long and making the biggest circles possible.
- 15 elbow circles: People laugh when they see these because I'm just standing there making big circles with my forearm, keeping the upper arm stationary. Do these with just a little bit of quickness and get your blood moving.
- 15-second wrist stretches against a wall: Just pressing the hands flat against a wall and locking the elbows, letting the joints get used to bending.
- PVC pipe snatch-grip overhead rotations: Grab a PVC pipe or stretching stick in your snatch grip and rotate it with the arms straight forward, over and behind. This one looks like you're missing a snatch behind you, only you're not taking your hands off the stick. It might be tough if you've got really tight shoulders, so you can move the hands out wider if you've got that problem.
- 20 side-to-side torso twists: Just simple twists, trying to get the shoulders as far as possible to the right and left on each rotation.
- 15 side bends: Nothing complicated here, just bending sideways at the hips to the left and right, knees stay straight.
- 20 wide-stance groin shifts: This is a name I made for this stretch. Just put your feet out wide to the sides, keep your knees straight, and shift your hips to the right and left, feeling the stretch in the opposite groin (when you shift to the right, the left groin is getting stretched). This is a movement stretch; you're going back and forth slowly.
- 10 knee kicks: Just stand there and kick your knee back and forth ten times, then do the other leg. Get full flexion and extension on each kick, and hang on to something to steady yourself if you start to lose your balance.
- 10 leg swings: Stand in front of a bar in a squat rack, grab the bar with your hands, and swing your leg back and forth like you're kicking an NFL field goal. Get the longest possible range here, your foot should come up to the level of the bar on the forward part of the swing.
- 15 second lunge groin stretches: One of the only static stretches I do before a workout, just getting into a lunge position and

pushing the hips forward to stretch the groin. Don't overstretch and tear something.

- 10 toe-touches with a PVC pipe or stretching stick: Simple, grab the stick in a clean grip and do ten toe-touches up and down, keeping the knees straight but not locked.
- 10 behind-the-neck presses with PVC pipe or stretching stick: Exactly like it sounds, just pressing up and down to full lockout.
- 10 back squats with a PVC pipe or stretching stick: Again, just like it sounds. Get that bottom position ready.
- 5 toe-touches with an empty barbell: Basically like a straight-leg deadlift.
- 5 behind-the-neck presses with an empty barbell: Simple.
- 5 back squats with an empty barbell: Now we're getting the bottom position looser with a little more weight than the PVC pipe.

That takes me about eight minutes, usually. I hustle through it, not stopping to chat with anybody or fiddle with my phone. After the last thing on the list, I load the bar with 50 kilos for my first set of snatches. As I said, that's the whole shebang. I've been using it for several years and I've probably had less pain and fewer little pulls and strains than even before.

Now, there are a couple of asterisks here. If I'm having particular tightness in a certain area, I'll add a little something to this order. A perfect example would be foam rolling on the IT bands. When this area starts to get tight, I use a foam roller on it for 5-6 reps before I get started. This type of thing would be in addition to the normal progression I listed here. I never leave anything out. I've seen a lot of lifters who have to use bands, tennis balls, and other little gadgets to loosen up tight shoulders, calves, or whatever. If you've got a problem area like this, you might just need to try out a few different techniques until you settle on a routine you like.

As you can probably see from looking at this, I think most of your warm-up routine should be movement-based. I don't like doing a lot of static stretching before lifting workouts. I say that because I used to do a LOT of static stretching before I trained, and it led to several minor injuries. We've read some research in recent years about how pronounced static stretching of a muscle prior to lifting can increase the chance of a strain or partial tear, but I didn't know this when I was a young athlete. I just stretched the same way I was taught in football practice, lots of stretch-and-hold-for-ten-seconds stuff. That was the only thing I had ever known.

Now, having learned so much over the years, I believe joint mobility is what you're aiming for when you're preparing to train and light ballistic movement is the best way to get it.

Just do it, seriously...

Everything I've suggested in this article will add about ten minutes to your workouts...total. I will absolutely bloody promise you that this will work, people. I do this every single time I train, exactly the way I've written it out here. I can verify from personal experience that you'll have less pain if you do these things.

You'll probably have fewer minor injuries too. The tightness that accumulates in your joints can build up to a point where you might actually change your technique in the snatch and clean and jerk without even realizing that you're doing it. This happens sometimes. Lifters are so stiff that they'll do anything to avoid the positions that lead to flaming, excruciating discomfort. Unintentionally, the athletes might make little tweaks to their technique because they're trying to stay away from those positions. Before you know it, you might have actually developed some technical problems in your lifts...all because you were in pain and you weren't doing the proper things to manage it. Then you've got a problem, Jack.

This is just one possible routine you could use to get your body ready for the barbell. There are a million other ways to do it, and any of them are fine if they accomplish the job for you personally. However, I think I'm on safe ground by saying that you'll definitely have to use some kind of warm-up prior to training. You won't be able to just blow this off when you're older. So regardless of how you choose to do it, the point is that some form of preparation will be a requisite.

Programming Phase Two: Exercise Selection

Which lifts should you be concentrating the most time and effort on? There are lots and lots of strength-building exercises associated with the barbell.

If you've got experience in this game, you've probably heard plenty of programming ideas from successful athletes and coaches. What this all boils down to is the fact that you've got an almost unlimited selection of lifts and movements you can use, and you need to pick the right ones. You especially need to pick the right ones when you're older, because your time is more limited and you don't want to waste any of it. Here are some basic categories to help you organize your training, and I've ranked them in order of importance:

The Competition Lifts

These are the full versions of the two main competitive OLifts: the snatch and the clean & jerk. Your development as a successful Olympic lifter will mainly depend on the technical skill you can develop in these lifts, so practicing them is the top priority in your training.

Squatting

Squatting is the most important assistance movement in Olympic weightlifting. The squat has often been referred to as the best developer of overall body strength that can be performed with a barbell. There might come a time in your older years when you can't use squats in training anymore because of physical limitations. You cross that bridge when you come to it, and we'll discuss possible alternatives to squatting later in this book. But you should try to continue squatting as long as possible into your weightlifting career. It's literally the best way to stay strong, period. Most Olympic lifters use two main forms:

- Back Squat
- Front Squat
- Variations such as pause squats (front or back squats performed with a short pause in the bottom position)

Pulling & Pressing Assistance Movements

These are lifts that are incorporated into an athlete's training program to improve pulling or overhead technique and strength without actually performing the full snatch or clean. Exercises include:

- Snatch Pulls
- Clean Pulls
- Snatch-grip or Clean-grip Deadlifts
- RDLs (Romanian Deadlifts)
- Push Press
- BTN (behind the neck) Push Press
- Snatch-grip BTN Push Press
- There are multiple other pulling/pressing exercises, along with several variations of the ones listed here.

Variants of the Competition Lifts

These are exercises that include some kind of movement directly connected with the SN or C&J, such as:

- Power Snatch
- Power Clean
- Rack Jerk
- Power Jerk
- Overhead Squat
- Snatch Balance
- Block work (performing variations of the snatch or clean from elevated blocks, making it a kind of partial movement)

Assistance Exercises not Directly Derived from the OLifts

These are general weight training movements that can help develop a lifter's overall strength level, but they are not as closely connected to the SN and C&J as the exercises from #2 and #3 above. These are exercises like:

- Military Press
- Bench Press
- Straight-leg Deadlift
- Arm exercises (bicep curls, tricep extensions, etc.)
- Glute-ham raises

Abdominal Exercises

This category needs special discussion. Even though we have it listed as the sixth priority on this list, abdominal work is tremendously important and should be incorporated into every one of your workouts. This is essential for improvement as a weightlifter and also for injury prevention. There is almost an unlimited assortment of abdominal exercises, such as:

- Sit-ups
- Crunches
- Hanging leg raises
- Plate twists
- Plank holds

These are the things that should comprise your training program. This list is based on my opinion and personal preference as a lifter/coach, by the way. Others might have different ideas about how their importance should be ordered. So, if these are the lifts we're supposed to do in training, how should they be arranged during a workout?

Programming Phase Three: Workout Exercise Order

Which lifts should be done first in a workout, and which ones should be done last? There are various perspectives on this, but here is a common ordering system that many coaches follow:

Speed lifts: Lifts that require the most explosiveness and speed should be performed first in the workout, when the body is freshest. In other words, the competition lifts and their variants go at the beginning.

Speed-strength lifts: These are lifts that still have a speed and explosiveness element to them, but they're also classified as strength developers because they aren't full competition lifts or variants. Pulling/pressing assistance movements fit this category.

Strength lifts: These are the exercises that are primarily used for strength development, such as squats and slower pulling movements (deadlifts, RDLs, etc.)

Secondary lifts: These are lifts from the *assistance exercises not directly derived from the OLifts* category, such as bench presses. Referring to these as "secondary lifts" doesn't mean they aren't important. They are. But they aren't as important as the other lifts that come before them.

Abdominal work: Ab work should go at the end of the workout, simply because that's the most sensible place to put it when you look at the big picture.

Programming Phase Four: Weekly Structure

Here is one of the most important considerations in the training of a masters weightlifter: *Older lifters will have to organize their training around the demands of their real life.* Young athletes don't have to worry about the kinds of commitments you have, so their training schedules can be planned with practically no restrictions. You're older, and that means you've got to think about your job, family, house payment, yard work, etc. And unless Bill Gates decides he wants to start using some of his billions to give full-time salaries to old weightlifters so we can all train without working for a living, it's probably going to stay this way.

However, I want to start this section by giving you a full-blown training program, just so we can see what a "best case scenario" looks like. *This is NOT a masters-specific program.* We'll get to those eventually. This is the kind of program you would use for young full-time weightlifters who are in the prime of their athletic lives and basically have the ability to devote their entire weekly schedule to training (aside from possibly going to school or working a few hours at a part-time job).

MONDAY

- Snatch
- Snatch Pulls
- Back Squat
- Ab work

TUESDAY

- Rack Jerk
- Power Clean or another variant (block work, snatch balance, etc.)
- Pressing exercises (military press, bench press, etc.)
- Ab work

WEDNESDAY

- Clean
- Clean Pulls
- Ab work

THURSDAY

- Snatch
- Snatch-grip Deadlift
- Front Squat
- Ab work

SATURDAY

- C&J
- Clean-grip Deadlift
- Pause Squats (back squat with a pause in the bottom position)
- Ab work

Background of this particular program: From 1993 through 2004, I trained in Washington with the Calpian weightlifting club, coached by John Thrush. The Calpian team was one of the powerhouses in US weightlifting back in those days. We won the National Team Championship in 2000 and were consistently ranked in the top two or three teams at every national meet we went to for 10-15 years. If you walked into our gym back in the 90s, it wasn't uncommon to see three or four national champions or world team members, along with multiple national-level competitors. Our club was extremely team-oriented, and most of our athletes were using a program very similar to the one I just outlined. I didn't create this method; John Thrush did. I trained with a program like this throughout the top years of my career, and I've also used it to coach other athletes I've worked with over the years. It's a proven system that has produced consistent success.

However, I've continued on as a competitive weightlifter beyond my 20s, into my 30s and 40s. I can definitely tell you that this program isn't for older athletes. First of all, it's a five-day program. Personally, I was able to handle this much training volume when I was in my teenage years and early-mid 20s. Almost every athlete in our club did the same. However, my body started having a lot of difficulty recovering from workouts when I was around 26-27. My joint pain increased quite a bit, and nagging little injuries like muscle pulls and strains were becoming more frequent. I spoke with John around this time, and we agreed to move me to a four-day program. It looked more like this:

MONDAY

- Snatch
- Snatch Pulls
- Back Squat
- Ab work

WEDNESDAY

- Rack Jerk
- Power Clean or another variant (block work, snatch balance, etc.)
- Pressing exercises (military press, bench press, etc.)
- Ab work

THURSDAY

- Clean
- Clean Pulls
- Front Squat
- Ab work

SATURDAY

- Snatch
- C&J
- Pause Squats (back squat with a pause in the bottom position)
- Ab work

As you can see, I added a day of rest (Tuesday) to allow more recovery. We were still able to keep approximately the same amount of work from the five-day program, but some things had to be dropped or rearranged. This was my training program from the age of 26 through 32. I continued to have a lot of success in competition, and I actually qualified to compete in the 2004 US Olympic Trials when I was 32.

After the 2004 Trials, I left Washington and moved to Arizona. I've remained a member of the Calpian team to this day, but I've been training myself since I moved. As I said, I was 32 when this change happened. When I moved to Arizona, I got a new job that was much more demanding and time-consuming than I had in Washington. The hectic new job, along with my age, basically forced me to completely rearrange how I trained. I decided to start training twice a week. Here is the program I've used for approximately the last eight years.

TUESDAY

- Snatch (light-moderate)
- C&J (light-moderate)
- Back Squat (heavy)
- Straight-leg Deadlift
- Ab work

SATURDAY

- Snatch (heavy)
- C&J (heavy
- Back Squat (light-moderate)
- Straight-leg Deadlift
- Ab work

I've described this program to a lot of people in recent years, and it always causes some raised eyebrows and funny looks. They see multiple problems with it, and here's what they usually are:

- Training twice a week isn't enough work to be a successful weightlifter.
- There are no pulls on the program.
- There are no front squats on the program.

Okay, those are all legitimate concerns. In fact, I'll address each one of them because I'm sure you want to know the logic behind this:

Training twice a week isn't enough work to be a successful weightlifter: Correct, training twice a week isn't enough work... for a younger lifter. As we've just seen, I did a lot more work when I was young. But everything changes when you're older, as we've constantly stated throughout this book. Part of the reasoning for training twice a week is simply job-related. With the hours I put in at work, I don't have time for much more than this. But even if my job weren't a factor, I would probably still be training twice a week because I've been doing it for almost ten years now and I've had success. My body has remained healthy and I've continued to lift some of the top weights in the country in my age division.

There are no pulls on the program: Because I have over 25 years of weightlifting experience at this point, I was able to eliminate pulls from my program without a negative effect on my lifting. As I got older, I found they were adding a lot of extra time to my workouts and also considerable soreness in my lower back. I decided to get rid of them basically as an experiment, just to see if my pulling strength and power would diminish. That hasn't happened. Since I've been able to lift successfully without them, I haven't added them back in and I have no plans to in the future.

There are no front squats on the program: My explanation for this is almost identical to what I just wrote about pulls. Front squats were simply putting a lot of wear and tear on my body, so I decided to get rid of them just to test the effect it would have on my lifting. I haven't encountered any significant problems as a result of eliminating them. But as with the pulls, I think the fact that I have extensive previous experience is part of the explanation for this. In other words, I think I've done enough pulls and front squats to last the rest of my life. That sounds like a joke, but there's actually some truth to it.

Straight-leg Deadlifts: I use these for injury prevention. When I was around 33, I developed some severe lower back pain. This was during the final few months of keeping pulls in my program. The pain was extreme to the point that I had to stop training for a short time. After taking some time off and speaking with a physical therapist, who gave me some remedial abdominal exercises to assist with the back problems, I started incorporating straight-leg deadlifts into my program simply to keep my lower back/hamstrings strong and flexible. I do three or four sets of five reps at the end of my workouts, with around 50% of the weight I use for back squats. So these aren't a heavy-weight exercise, and they aren't supposed to be. Personally, I've found they keep my back healthy. It's a totally individual training addition.

Once again, I'm going to use something I've previously written to illustrate the material we're analyzing. This is an excerpt from a short article I wrote for the Catalyst Athletics blog called "A Masters Weightlifting Program That Worked." This is a chance for you to see my two-day program in action. I've used it for all of my competitions since 2005, and this is a look at how it led to one of my top performances as a masters lifter.

A Masters Weightlifting Program That Worked

Excerpt from Catalyst Athletics website May 21st 2014

This is a program I designed and used to prepare for one of my own meets in 2008. I've included several notes so it'll make sense, because it's not written in a way you would normally see in a regular program.

There are many ways to design a successful training program. Nobody has the market cornered in this department. This is an example of something that worked well for me, so there should be something you can learn from it. Other people train much differently, and that's fine. This is just another addition to your knowledge base, and hopefully it'll provide some food for thought.

This is a 14-week program I followed while training for the 2008 American Masters. There are several factors to mention with this program:

- I was 36 years old at this time and I trained twice a week (Tuesday and Saturday).
- The only lifts I put on the program were SN, C&J, and BSQ because these were the only ones that needed a loading plan. Assistance exercises like RDLs weren't necessary to program weights for.
- Only top weights of the day are listed, no warm-ups. Everything is in kilos.
- I was doing no front squats at all during this time. They caused too much wear and tear on my body and I was able to get all the leg strength I needed from back squats.

- Weights are listed as SN/C&J/BSQ. So, when looking at the program, something like 90/110/140x3 means the workout was:
  - Work up to a 90 kilo SN for at least a single, maybe two or three singles.
  - Work up to a 110 C&J, same manner as the snatch.
  - Work up to 140x3 in the BSQ
  - Remaining assistance, like RDLs and core work, isn't included with this loading progression.
- I planned two deloading weeks into the program to allow more recovery and avoid overtraining.
- Prior to starting this program, my personal records in the master's division were: SN: 137 kg, C&J: 163 kg, Total: 300 kg
- My lifetime PRs were 155 SN and 185 C&J, but those were from 10 years earlier.
- The first few weeks of the program were deliberately very light because I was coming off a layoff period and I felt like I needed to gradually ease back into training instead of ripping into big lifts right away.

14-week loading program:

	Tues. **(SN/C&J light, BSQ heavy)**		**Sat.** **(SN/C&J heavy, BSQ light)**
Week 1	60/90/140x3		80/110/110x3
Week 2	70/100/160x3		90/120/150x3
Week 3	80/110/180 2x3		100/130/170x3
Week 4	85/115/190 2x3		110/140/170x3
Week 5	70 SN/120 BSQ	**Deload**	100 C&J/140 BSQ
Week 6	75/105/195x3		100/145/150x3
Week 7	80/110/200x3		120/120/160x3
Week 8	85/115/205x2		100/150/180x3
Week 9	90/120/210x1		125/120/185x1
Week 10	70 SN/120 BSQ	**Deload**	100 C&J/140 BSQ
Week 11	80/110/200x2		100/155/180x2
Week 12	90/120/207.5x2		130/120/190x2
Week 13	90/120/185x1		120/140/185x1
Week 14	*Meet Week- BSQ up to 150x2 on Tuesday, compete Sunday*		

Meet, 2008 American Masters Championship, Savannah, GA

SNATCH	CLEAN & JERK
1st attempt: 125	1st attempt: 145
2nd attempt: 133	2nd attempt: 155
3rd attempt: 138	3rd attempt: 165

TOTAL: 303

Six-for-six, 1st place 105+ class and Best Lifter 35-39 age group, new master's division personal records in each lift

Additional training notes

- Once I passed the first four weeks ("getting back in shape" time period), I started alternating light SN/heavy C&J every Saturday. Heavy work in both competition lifts was not done on the same day to avoid overtraining.
- Tuesday (light day) weights were not selected according to any specific percentage protocol. I simply chose weights that would give me some good work without fatiguing me for Saturday. Being 36 years old and having almost twenty years of muscle memory in the SN and C&J made lots of heavy training attempts counter-productive.
- Heavy squatting was kept 2-3 weeks away from the competition.
- At first glance, some of you might be saying, "This doesn't look like much work." My response is, "That's correct, but you need to understand a few things." A) I usually work between 60-70 hours a week at my job, so I don't have time for much more than this. B) At 36 years old, I didn't need much more work than this. It might not look productive on paper, but it produced terrific results. C) Here's a quote from Norb Schemansky, one of the greatest weightlifters of all time: *"Don't attempt maximums in the gym. Some members of the U.S. lifting team couldn't believe how much more I could do in a contest, where it counted. I was never burned out. Attempts at limit weights should be restricted to once every three or four weeks. One should not work any more than 80 to 90% of his limit in training."*

This is a demonstration of how the two-day program was put into action. Once again, it's important to remember that I designed this program for myself, nobody else. It was a completely individual decision that incorporated all the aspects of my own lifting experience, needs, restrictions, etc. I had to build it myself because, as we've said from the beginning, I couldn't find any reliable, sensible information about how to train at an older age. In other words, a program like this might work for you…and it might not. However, looking at it is a good illustration of this fundamental law:

The training program you use as a master will have to blend two main factors:

- The things *you personally need to do* in training to be successful.
- The things *you're personally capable of doing* in training that will keep you healthy.

That leads us to internal conversations like this:

Self: "I've got a bunch of different things I need to do in training every week (full lifts, squats, pulls, block work, bench press, hang movements, pressing assistance). I need to train five or six days a week if I want to fit all this stuff in."

Response from your brain: "You're 46. If you train heavy five or six days a week, you'll probably get hurt. And even if you don't get hurt, you'll be in constant pain."

At this point, do you listen to your brain? Many people don't. It absolutely blows me away how weightlifting can cause intelligent human beings to almost completely abandon common sense. They know they're doing too much and they need to back off, but they won't do it. Even when they're hurting, injured, not making progress and putting up crappy performances in meets, they still insist on doing things the same way. I'm going to hit you with some deep Confucian-type wisdom here:

If you have a consistent way of doing things, and your results are consistently poor, that means your way of doing things needs to be changed.

But if you don't want to listen to me, fine. Keep banging your head against the brick wall. Either the wall will fall down or you'll crack your skull open and slip into a coma. Either way, I guess the problem is solved.

So this is some input on training programs from one individual who has had success as an older lifter. What I want to do now is move to another section where we explore the programs of other lifters who have also accomplished tremendous things beyond 30.

Programming Phase Five: Training Analysis of Elite Masters Lifters

When I was putting together my ideas for this book, I decided it was important to include as many diverse opinions as possible. In the previous pages, you've seen how Matt Foreman trains and what works for him as an older lifter. However, we've established the concept that masters OLifting is a highly personalized pursuit. Knowing this, you need to see more than one man's perspective on it.

Fortunately, some of the best masters athletes in the United States (and the world) agreed to share their beliefs about training with us. The following section is a collection of interviews I did with these individuals. All of them responded in their own way to the questions I asked. With a few of these interviews, I was able to simply stick them in here word-for-word because their responses were direct and needed very little editing. In some other cases, I had to rearrange their answers to accommodate the kind of analysis we need. However, all of the information you're going to read is factual and straight from the mouths of these champion lifters. Let's take a look.

Athlete: Fred Lowe

Birth Year: 1947
Weight Class: 62-85 kg

- Three-time Olympian (1968, 1972, 1976)
- Eight-time US National Champion (1969-1981)
- US National Record Holder
    - 182.5 kg C&J (402 lbs) at 75 kg bodyweight (165 lbs), 1981
- Nine-time World Masters Champion

- World Masters Record Holder
  - 130 kg C&J (286 lbs) at 69 kg bodyweight (152 lbs), 50-54 age group
- National Masters Champion (1993-present)
- National Masters Record Holder (multiple weight classes and age groups)
  - 140 kg C&J (308 lbs) at 77 kg bodyweight (169 lbs), 50-54 age group
  - 85 kg snatch (187 lbs) at 69 kg bodyweight (152 lbs), 65-69 age group

When I decided to write a book about masters weightlifting, I knew right away that I wanted to include a section of training information directly from highly successful masters lifters. As soon as I made this decision, the first name that went on my list was Fred Lowe. I made sure I pestered him for some of his thoughts and ideas, because Fred is one of the greatest weightlifters in American history. A three-time Olympic team member in 1968, 1972, and 1976, Fred broke American records and won national championships until he decided to give it a rest in the 1980s. When he got the itch to compete again in the 1990s as a master, the same old story just repeated itself. Fred has continued to win and break records every time he steps on the platform, and we're honored to have his contributions in this book.

Interview: As far as weightlifting is concerned, I am 67 years old. Back in the day, I competed on and off between the ages of 18-35, including three Olympic Games appearances. After a ten-year absence, I decided to come back to compete in 1993 at age 46. I had waited until I thought the time was right. In 1993, for various reasons, the time was right for me. I have had one hell of a lot of fun doing this again, and I've been at it as a master for the better part of 22 years non-stop.

When you decide to lift as a master, there are a few things you have to come to terms with (guys particularly). If you don't, you won't last long. I've worked up a list of things that have enabled me to stick with the sport again for the 22 years since I came back to it.

FREDDY'S "COME TO TERMS" LIST

1. You are not the person you were. Guys, if you compete long enough, you will eventually embody that Stone Temple Pilots lyric "I'm half the man I used to be." Even though this will

inevitably become the case, you'll still be a BADASS for your age. None of your same-age non-lifting friends will be as functional. This will be its own reward (unless some huge business has called you up to offer sponsorship). As you work your way up through the age groups, the physical adjustments become more numerous and they're all crucial to your continued participation.

2. You are not as strong as you used to be. You can still maximize it for your age and ability, but it will not be the same as back in the day. Don't put in a lot of time and energy lamenting this, and don't live in the past (it results in boring conversations—I don't have a time machine and we can't go back—ignore Eddie Money's "I Wanna Go Back, and Do It All Over" on this one). The jumps between sets in training will be smaller.
3. You are not as flexible as you used to be. This is a category that you will have to work on just as hard as strength and technique. Work it *really* hard at the end of the workout when you're at your hottest and most pliable. Yeah, I know you already feel great from your Geezer workout, but I don't care. Don't neglect this piece; if you do, you won't maximize your results.
4. If you act stupidly and do this wrong, the consequences are generally more egregious than in your younger years. Have a general framework in mind for your training, but be intuitive and listen to your body. If it's not a good day, dial it back but be as thorough as you can. You will still be happy (you'll feel just like the Pharrell Williams song "Happy").
5. Something is always better than nothing. The good news is that nothing is set in stone, and your body will never lie to you. Now, review #4.
6. Three days per week at some level of effort is a great frequency for the master lifters. Truth be told, Chad Vaughn got a lifetime competition PR while training three days per week at age 31, and that's not even masters age. What makes you think you need to train 4-6 days per week anyway?
7. Your training has *nothing* to do with Bulgaria, China, or Russia. It has to do with YOU and the current state of your strength, technique, and range of motion. Don't overcomplicate things...work on basics and be consistent. There's no secret and no magic bullet.

8. If continuing to do these lifts is a priority for you, then save whatever physical capability you have left for the platform. If you train regularly you won't need any other sports to stay in shape, and just about all the others are *dangerous*. So, decide what's really important to you.
9. Back squatting may not be as comfortable now if you've lost any fluid volume in your spinal discs. Plentiful water intake is crucial for all your body systems. If you don't have a good history of this, try to start with 8 glasses of water/day and work up to half your bodyweight in ounces per day. Now you can view *water as a food supplement*. You're a lifter, right? You must like supplements! Well, water is the cheapest, and it's the best one. Yeah, I know that the taste is boring. Just quit bitching about all of these inconveniences in your life to accommodate something you supposedly really care about. Artificial colorings/flavorings to make things more interesting? Well, after all, your liver weighs SIX pounds so it'll handle a lot!
10. If back squats now hurt your back or neck, do front squats. If front squats hurt, do dumbbell squats pre-exhausted with leg presses (if you have a machine). Or, just do complexes where you squat clean and then do any number of extra recoveries. Then, try to jerk that shit! It feels like a world record, even though it isn't. Modify ANY training you do to pay homage to things that aren't very comfortable. With the modifications comes your best WORK. This is what it's all about. When you walk into a training session, you are there to do as much WORK as you are capable of within your ROM and your energy level for that day.
11. Get as much sleep as you need. If you think you can train for weightlifting now and adequately recover without adequate rest, then it's even more ridiculous than when you tried to do it when you were younger.
12. Most of the training that I do is between 50-85% of my *reasonable* goals for the next meet. I am a believer in cyclical percentages short and long-term and feel they likely should trend lighter the older you get. My method of training is to set the percentages for the cycle and then execute things according to how I feel in this manner: if I feel good, I adhere to the scheduled percentage. If I don't feel good or if something is nagging

> me, I dial things back but train very thoroughly and work flexibility hard at the end. In this way, I get a decent workout no matter how I feel. I don't ever go any heavier than scheduled, even if I feel good. It doesn't count in my basement. If I haven't got enough confidence to lift more in competition than I do in training by this point, I might as well give it all up right now. I prefer to go all out (basement inspired) about 10 days before the meet. That's the only time I'll ever be (hopefully) over 85% of my targets. How much would I care to beat myself up anyway? I'm trying to just keep going in the first place. Now, review #5.

I could go on and on, and someday I'm sure I will (well, actually, I'm working on something quite long-winded but hopefully interesting). But for our purposes here, this is roughly how I go about it.

This approach has allowed me to set world masters records in several different weight classes and age divisions. It's true that I have the gift, but it's also true that I can't utilize the gift if I'm so bashed up that I can't train or compete. As a master, you can take things as seriously as you care to.

It's a free country and you can get as fired up about this part of your lifting career as you care to. Tell all the naysayers to get off their asses and start doing something other than massaging their keyboards. However you do this, though, you will derive more benefit from the time you put into it than anything else you could think of…just be sensible and don't go off half-cocked.

To all of you masters…train hard and train smart. I love you all—each and every one. Keep movin' that shit! Happy training!

Athlete: Rick Bucinell

Birth Year: 1964
Weight Class: +105 kg

- World Masters Champion
- World Masters Record Holder
  - 143 kg snatch (315 lbs), 45-49 age group
- National Masters Champion
- National Masters Record Holder
  - 188 kg C&J (414 lbs), 335 kg total (738 lbs), 40-44 age group

- 150 kg snatch (330 lbs), 190 C&J (418 lbs), 340 kg total (749 lbs), 45-49 age group

Rick Bucinell is an interesting case study because he didn't start training the Olympic lifts until he was 39 years old. Those of you who are coming late to this party can draw a lot of inspiration from his story, because he has risen to the title of World Champion in less than ten years. The lifts he has done in competition in his 40s can compete evenly with most of our country's top athletes, even in the younger divisions. Here's a look at his methods.

Interview: Thanks for the opportunity to help out and offer up some of my training insight. I think to understand how I train, you have to know where I come from.

I was a HIIT trainer for many years prior. After much hesitation, my good friend and coach Morgan Norval got me to try the lifts for the first time at the age of thirty-nine, and I was hooked. A bit late, but what can I say? You may not know Morgan by name, but his deeds in USAW are pretty well known. Morgan provides the funding for the Jennifer Roy Award for young lifters in USAW. Because we both came from the HIIT style, which calls for longer rest periods between training sessions of muscle groupings due to high central nervous system recruitment, we knew that rest between heavier sessions was the key to progress for me rather than daily training. Now that I was approaching 40 years old with a busy schedule, this became even more important. I guess you can say my HIIT training years were my warm-up for my Olympic style training years.

My typical cycles are broken up into out-of-competition cycles and competition-prep cycles, with mini-cycles mixed in. Out-of-competition prep cycles consist of more strength and slower movements, heavy pulls, presses, and weak strength areas that we feel need work. Of course there are always squats, lots of front squats.

Personally, I'm not a fan of back squats. The late Mike Cady once told me during a discussion on squatting, "If you can front squat it three times, you should be able to clean it." I've come to find that may not be true, but it's a hell of a motivator. Back squats tend to put me in a position that is less conducive to a good technical Olympic lifting position. Bent over at the waist is a position I see with many heavy squatters. This may allow them to squat heavy, but what is it doing to reinforce their rack position in a heavy clean or bottom position in a snatch? There are good high-bar squatters of course, but you don't see it that often in masters lifters. Many are sacrificing good squatting posture to lift heavier weight. Please don't think I'm trashing back squats. You must keep in mind, I train twice a week and need to get the most effective work in as possible to transfer to my lifts.

My competition cycles are typically 16 weeks. I will do one of the lifts as the primary for the day and the second will be done for accessory work. Working on triples, doubles and complexes with the primary lift and your most effective accessories: pulls, rack jerks, and snatch balance with variations as needed. I will do these from varying positions, whether from blocks or the hang. I use percentages based strictly on how I feel that day. As a masters lifter, every day is not your best day. When I have ignored this in the past, it has led to injuries that set my training back days, or even weeks.

My percentages are always on the high side after the first 2 weeks. I like to work heavy. I feel working between 75 and 90 percent is best for me. This gives me good feel for the bar and I can't slack on the technique. My warm-ups to my percentages for the day are always using my competition warm-up progressions. Although I may be using different percentages, the body knows what's coming on the way there.

Weeks 6 through 10, I start doing my front squats first. I love this part of the cycle because my squats really start to go up. Granted, your legs are trashed when it comes to the lifts, but it pays big dividends when they recover. A typical day during this period would look like this:

FSQ: 80% 180kg x 3 x 4 sets

Snatch: 80% 112kg x2 x 4sets

Clean Pulls: 90% (pull RPM) 180kg x 2 x 4 sets

Weeks 11 through 13, I'll perform both full lifts during the sessions. Working percentages are between 80% and 95%. This helps to work out the bugs and to get in shape to handle the heavy loads on competition day. Sets range between 3 and 5 for singles at the working percentages for the day. I never perform a max lift in training. Schemansky alluded to this in his writing. Personally, I don't get the adrenaline rush in training I get in competition needed to attempt a maximum. During these three weeks, I will sometimes schedule workouts with guys in the area known to lift heavy weights for the push. Front squats are now done at the end of the sessions in order to focus on the lifts.

Weeks 14 and 15, I start to back off on the total volume in order to recover. Nothing above what might be my second attempt, two singles of each lift. No squats—this gives the legs a chance to recover.

Week 16: I work up to what would be my opening attempt for two singles. I try to give myself two solid days of rest before a competition.

In terms of recovery, I am a huge fan of massage and chiropractic. Prior to a competition, I get a massage every three weeks and as I get closer, it goes to every week. I use chiropractic as needed, usually receiving adjustments every two to three weeks.

Keep in mind I only get to train 2 sessions per week. What I have outlined is my typical cycle of training for the last 11 years. Only minor changes have been made and it's kept me out of the doctor's office.

Athlete: Corinne Grotenhuis

Birth Year: 1965
Weight Class: 63 kg

- American Open Champion
- World Masters Champion
- Pan American Masters Champion
- National Masters Champion
- National Masters Record Holder
    - 66 kg snatch (145 lbs), 80 kg C&J (176 lbs), 146 kg total (321 lbs), 40-44 age group
    - 60 kg snatch (132 lbs), 45-49 age group

The first US National Championship for women was held in 1981. Corinne Grotenhuis made her debut on the national scene in 1984 and never looked back. She has the longest competitive career of any female OLifter in this country. Her success continued through her 20s and 30s as she graduated into the masters division, eventually becoming a World Champion and being inducted into the US Masters Hall of Fame. Here, she tells us about the many victories and challenges she has encountered along the road.

Interview: I started lifting when I was 15 under Mike Huszka. I wanted to be a bodybuilder, but I did not know better so he said he had to get me strong first. That was 33 years ago that I started Olympic lifting. Mike's workouts consisted of a pyramid always for 2 sets, going up x2. Squats were done daily and duck walking was also practiced for the rare occasion it was and is needed. Sit-ups were mandatory and we had to do over 200 at each workout. I added some bodybuilding moves, since I still wanted to be a bodybuilder. However, I was still competing in swimming, so I continued to cross train. I think the cross training has been the most successful part of my career. I have always done something else to prevent overuse and burnout.

During the period of age 15-20, in the summers I would train 2 times a day/3 times a week. I would still maintain training 6 days/week, all workouts average about 70-85% until it got closer to a meet and then, of course, my lifts would go up. Mike moved when I was 20, so then I joined Sayre Park and Roger Nielsen became my coach. Roger used the Bulgarian method with me and I would have to do the Russian squat routine periodically. During this time, I was not competing in swimming as I graduated high school and was in undergraduate studies. In this time, I still did bodybuilding, but my knees were fine then and I would run 5 miles, 3-4 times a week.

At Sayre Park, it was awesome since I got to train with Mike Karchut, Rich Schutz, Paul Fleschler, and Jeff Michels. Mike Karchut had built blocks at 6 different levels. Due to my size I stayed on 3 of the blocks and worked on speed getting under the bar from the different levels. During this period, my lifts were more at 85-90% and a lot of power moves. Reps were only 1-2 reps. Pulls were always at least 110%. A lot of 3-position moves were done during the week and on weekends it was snatch and clean and jerk to the max. I still trained 6 days a week.

Running stopped due to the stress it was beginning to cause my knees. I continued to do bodybuilding and added swimming and walking.

There was a period when I was training at 100% all the time. I had awesome lifts at that time, but I also had so much joint pain. The problem with this is that training at 100% is what I thought I had to do to be a good lifter despite hurting so much.

Mike Gattone ran the 1996 Olympics and said he would be moving back home afterwards. That is when Mike began to coach me. At this time, I was almost 30 years old. Mike's workouts were different. They were pyramids as well, but only 70-80%. Ironically, my pain disappeared because I was no longer training at such a high intensity. Mike had to constantly reassure me that I would still be able to compete at a high level when the time came. He was right. I would increase my lifts one month before the meet and it would always work. I have always been a lifter who lifts at least 2-5 kg more in a meet than in training, which is how it should be.

The workouts with Roger and Mike would be done for at least two months at a time before they would be changed. When Mike was coaching me, he would always put extra exercises in my workout to supplement my lifting, such as lunges, muscle snatches, muscle cleans, etc. This is when my first surgery began. At age 30, I tore my meniscus for the first time. It was also the first time I got 4th place at Nationals, even with a high total.

I took the entire year off for the torn meniscus, until Mike said, "Get going, it's time to start lifting." This time, I dropped down to 4 workouts per week, and only did full lifts. I no longer did power moves as my knees were beginning to hurt.

I specifically made sure I did rehab exercises for my knees daily and continued to do cross training with swimming, dragon boat racing, and canoe racing. My lifts continued to increase.

After each meet, I would analyze what I did right or wrong and, based on that, make the changes in the gym for the next meet. I usually do not miss a lift due to it being heavy, only by technical error. Every lift in the meet is usually easy, or used to be

When Roger Nielsen moved back to my area, he went back to coaching me again. Mike focused on sports performance and he was busy with the Chicago Bulls at that time.

I focused on a lot of overhead movements: push press, jerks and jerks behind the neck. Pulls were also heavy at 110%. Squatting went down to 2-3 times a week, and I only did 2-3 reps due to the first surgery.

My second arthroscopic surgery was about 3-4 years later. This time, I did not wait a year to resume training, only a few months. This was okay as I was able to maintain 4 days per week of training. But at this time, my hips were now higher up due to limited ability of bending. Oddly enough, at age 35 I was able to still lift like I did when I was younger, and I was still quite strong.

I never stopped cross training and bodybuilding, and I also began to start using supplements since I was getting older and figured I needed it.

I was able to still train with the passion and desire I had as a kid and was able to still train with the younger kids. When I hit my 40s, my focus changed a little. Squatting went down to 2 times per week and full lifts were done only once per week. I continued to cross train and rehab every day. My focus at this point was to compete in 22 Senior Nationals and be the only one in history to do this, and I did.

I knew I would not be able to qualify for nationals anymore, so I started to referee. I fell and tore my meniscus again, and this would now be the third scope on the knee. At this point, I did not let my knee heal as I wanted to compete in the World Masters Championships in Poland. I lifted with less than half range of motion. Once I won, I backed off and did my rehab. But the damage was done

At this point, I was now down to 3-4 days a week of training as I was now over 45 years old. Pulls had to be done from the hang only and flat feet. Squats were also down to 1-2 week and could only do 1-2 reps. Due to the knee pain progressing, I had to change what I did in the gym and tried to focus on what would maintain my strength. Pulls and overhead work were done a lot, as well as a lot of rehab. Over the course of 13 years I have tried every type of anti-inflammatory out there. I can no longer use any of them anymore as my body has become immune to them after so long.

Lifting was suffering and was painful. I was used to training for 33 years with lifting pain, but it had gotten to be not fun anymore and quality of life was no longer there. Other women were now beating me and I could no longer fight to stay on top, and honestly I was not used to losing.

I made the decision that I would have my last meet at the American Masters in 2013 and have a total knee replacement. Three scopes were no longer helpful and it was causing more harm than good. Rehab was not helping and I was scared that the Tylenol and anti-inflammatory meds were eating away at my liver.

I started to referee to stay close to the sport I love. Now I have this total knee replacement, but it is not healing the way it should. I will be allowed to lift, but instead of the 6-month wait I thought I needed, it will be a year.

What do I tell master lifters now? I stress the importance of cross training and bodybuilding. I stress core since I was taught so young to do no fewer than 200 sit-ups per day. I do not tell them 200, but will share at least 100. I will tell them that training 3-4 times a week is enough since we do not recover fast anymore, and it is much slower. I stress overhead movements and pulls at our age, and full lifts are not really needed when a meet is not near. Smaller jumps between attempts are more helpful, as it seems the larger jumps in attempts just don't work in our older years.

After every knee surgery and every meet, I re-analyze what was positive or not and make changes.

Athlete: Mike Gray

Birth Year: 1972
Weight Class: 105 kg

- American Open competitor at 40 years old
- 137 kg snatch (302 lbs)
- 151 kg C&J (332 lbs)
- 288 kg total (634 lbs)

Mike Gray began Olympic weightlifting when he was 34 years old, only one year away from officially being classified as a master. As he will describe in this interview, he has actually chosen not to register himself as a masters competitor throughout his lifting career. Mike makes the decision to register and compete head-to-head with senior division athletes (21-34 years old), age be damned. His best official snatch is actually 8 kilos above the current National Masters Record in his age division (40-44). We've talked a lot about not letting age restrict what you do as a weightlifter. Here's a look at a guy who simply refuses to acknowledge the restrictions of age, period.

Interview: I basically started Olympic weightlifting at 34. I had always lifted weights since I was 16, but I would call what I was doing "Power Beach," meaning the bigger movements like bench, squat and deadlifts with plenty of time hanging around a preacher bench. So having 8 years in Olympic lifting as I write this, I have definitely gone through my adjustments. My first 1.5 years were awesome. I could have done anything and gotten better. I would say most people are like this. In the years after that, people either get better or end up quitting as the progression rate slows.

I tried a "Bulgarian" style for about 18 months after my initial 18 months. It worked well at first, then it didn't. Once it stopped working, the injuries started to really pile up and I was too thick skulled to stop. The biggest adjustment I have made is really working with Greg Everett on my programming and bumping up a weight class. Once I had dumped the idea of becoming the next Zlaten Vanev and stopped maxing out every other day, I started paying attention to the other lifts as well, which of course meant pulls and squats to shore up my many weaknesses. Greg's programs have been great to me over the years and I've always had some success with them.

For my first 6 years, I was a starved 94 kg lifter, at 6'1. This was a bit silly, but I really wanted some success at that weight. After bombing out at the American Open in 2011, I decided I couldn't make that weight anymore. I bumped up to the 105 class, and it has been nothing but great ever since. My total went up and I feel I recover more than ever before. I also don't look like I am being sawed in half by the bar on every lift.

I train 5 days a week, Monday through Thursday and then Saturday. Monday and Wednesday I squat in the AM and do the rest after work. The reason for this is it helps me get loose and breaks up the day's work some. Tuesday and Thursday tend to be somewhat easier than the other days, concentrating more on speed and overhead issues. Saturday is just a 3-hour kick in the ass.

My warm up is the only non-organized thing in my training; it varies day-to-day depending on how I feel. I do bar complexes depending on the movements I have. So for example, if I am starting with snatches, I will do plenty of snatch Sots presses and snatch balances with the bar or very little weight. I don't like rolling around on dog toys and try to keep my warm up short and specific.

My volume is based heavily with my programming; Greg breaks up my training in 4 week cycles. Weeks 1-2 are chock full of volume, week 3 tends to be a testing week and the 4th week is backed off. Obviously the last 4 weeks before a meet changes, but it's basically the same.

I am a firm believer in the motto "If it's a lift you don't want to do, then it's a lift you probably should be doing." There isn't much I have an aversion to except power snatches. I don't like them because it changes up my technique some with me trying to keep above parallel, so those are out. I do back and abs every day, beach type work at least 3 times per week. Something that I really like is that Greg puts in plenty of combo work with a front squat sandwiched in there. It lets me sneak up squat volume without noticing it. An example would be front squat for a double + jerk or power clean + front squat + jerk. That stuff really works well for me.

I can't help anyone with pain management. I'm in pain most days. Some days are okay, and some days I question how much longer I can do this. I try to keep my NSAID use low, but I still use them. I like contrast showers, chiropractors, stretching in a pool, etc. Massage and restorative work laying on various devices don't do a damn thing for me.

It's one of the things I have accepted over the years that it's just a part of the game. When I first started, my wrists hurt so bad I had to dunk them in ice every night after I left Mike Burgener's gym. I remember thinking, "I can't stop this because I just dropped $200 on shoes."

Another funny thing…a few years ago I got the flu, the kind that drops you on the floor for 5 days. I remember lying there praying for death, and then I thought, "Damn, my knees feel good because I haven't trained in 4 days."

I have never thought as myself as a "masters" lifter, nor have I ever entered as one. I pay for a senior membership and compete as one. For me, this is a huge deal, as I think it makes me more hungry and competitive. I'm in the Navy and I work predominately with people much younger than me. I also train with people much younger than me. This is a huge component in my success as well, as it forces me to keep going harder and harder every day so I don't feel like I am losing a step on them. Younger people have and will beat me. It definitely happens, but I am going to make some of them really work for it.

I think people try to put a cap on how much they can lift if they enter the sport late. I understand there is a cap, but what you need to do is pull the IWF masters world records and take a hard look at it.

I would be in the 40-44 age group, 105 kg class if I competed as a master. The records for that class? Dzmitry Areshka owns that with a 152 kg snatch (335 lbs), 190 C&J (418 lbs) and a 342 kg total (753 lbs). That would've taken second or even first in the last 5 US National Championships (Seniors, not Masters). That tells me everything I need to know about limitations.

Masters have advantages over younger athletes, in my opinion. We are more focused than most, and we don't have to worry about food or rent as much as they do. I also don't have to share a hotel room with five other dudes at a meet.

The thing that I constantly think about being an older lifter is that my margin of error is nil. I have to be perfect in damn near everything I do. I don't have the room for error a 22 year-old may have. If I go out and get slammed drunk one night, I might be performing at less than optimal for a few days, whereas a 22 year-old won't. You just don't have as much daylight as they do, so you need to make the most of it.

Here is a big one; you need support. My wife, kids, friends, etc. are huge supporters of my lifting and me. My wife is absolutely incredible with this. She lets me train, lets me make my idiotic meals and fill the fridge with endless plastic containers, and doesn't say a word. She is so awesome with my lifting. Honestly, with all the success I've had, she was right there. It took me 5 years to get to the American Open. I was close a couple of times and the total kept shifting to the right, and I had a surgery in there as well on my knee, etc. Anyway, when I finally qualified after taking a freaking beating for 5 years, it was a huge feat for me. As I came off the platform, I hugged Greg, headed out to the parking lot to get some air, and she was just standing there with a cold Tecate in her hand, smiling. I swear to god, I almost lost it. It was such a great day for me and I will never forget it.

When I proposed to her, of course I got down on one knee. After she said yes, she immediately said, "Will you please get up? That has to be killing your knees." That's the kind of support I have.

Athlete: Jodi Stumbo

Birth Year: 1966
Weight Class: 75 kg

- National Masters Champion
- Pan American Masters Champion
- National Masters Record Holder:
    - 68 kg snatch (149 lbs), 81 kg C&J (178 lbs), 149 kg total (328 lbs), 45-49 age group
- World Masters Record Holder:
    - 68 kg snatch (149 lbs)

Jodi Stumbo is the type of weightlifter you don't see very often. Her experience in the sport goes back to the 90s. However, unlike many masters lifters, she has actually done the highest lifts of her career in her 40s. Most of the time, people who have OLifting experience going back to their 20s are lifting lighter weights when they're in their 40s, even if they have success in the masters division. Jodi has done the highest weights of her career so far in her masters years, even more than she did 10 years earlier. Obviously she has found a way to train successfully, and we're happy to take a look at her story.

Interview: I started lifting in 1994 when I joined a gym in Santa Fe, NM. Carl Miller was the owner and introduced me to weightlifting. His son, Shane Miller, and I were training partners from the start. Whatever he snatched, I would have to clean and jerk. Shane Miller became my coach at that time and has been my coach since. I went to nationals in 1996 in the 70 kg class and at that time by best lifts were 62.5 kg and 72.5 kg. Then I had a few kids and was back up to training by 2000. I did local meets in that time frame, but not National meets.

By 2003, my best lifts were 67.5 kg and 82.5 kg at age 37 at a bodyweight of 73 kg. My lifts in 2013-2014 are 68 and 83 at a bodyweight of 73 kg.

When I first started to lift, I would do snatches one day with some assistance exercises like clean deadlift, back squats and push presses. And then the next day I would do cleans, and then jerks off the rack. Mostly I would do

5 or 6 sets of low reps like 2-3. It wasn't based off a percentage system, but what felt like increased load.

I would prepare for competitions by doing the Cluster training system that broke it down by how many weeks out you were. It was divided into Prep phase (5 to 8 weeks) and Contest phase (4 to 5 weeks). The first was based on the idea of overload and some partial movements. The Contest phase was overload and whole movements with a peaking week. I would train 4 days a week. First day is snatch, snatch pulls and SDL (snatch-grip deadlift) and front squats. Next day clean and jerks, clean pulls, CDL (clean-grip deadlift) and back squats. The third day was snatch, clean and jerk, snatch pulls and then clean pulls. The fourth day was jerk from the rack, heavy jerk partial movement, SDL and CDL, and my choice of squats. Normally the reps and sets were 4/5 sets of 2/3 reps. My warm up sets were included in the count.

Now I use a percentage of my lifts and do not count my warms up into my daily reps. My training cycles are about 8 to 10 weeks long. This year I would train the lifts as close to 100% for a single every fifth workout. The other days I would perform 60% of my max for multiple reps. I would alternative the heavy lifts every fifth workout. My deadlifts would be 108% if I was going 60% in the lifts. Because of my knees, I stopped squatting all together. I stopped front squatting in 2010 due to a meniscus tear. Every time I would go below parallel, my knee would blow up. Before the 2011 National Masters, I had to do power snatches and power cleans for months. Then my coach, Shane Miller, suggested I switch to split cleans. I helped my knee so much that when I was in the warm up room before the meet, I was thinking of switching back to squat style. But everyone rolled their eyes as this suggestion and told me to split. I still do sort of a power snatch to this day. For a while I would back squat up to about 70/80 kg for 5 sets of 3, but now I can't do that. I try to keep my leg strength with good morning, RDLs and heavy deadlifts.

In the fall of 2013, I went back to the 4 day a week program. Since my last child entered kindergarten, it was time to add back that day and really try to make some gains in my lifting.

My warm up is cardio work for about 10 minutes, but lately 20 minutes on the bike for my knees, along with pull downs, air squats, and PVC pipe for motion. This takes me about 30 minutes.

I don't count the light reps with bar. I start at 25 kilos regardless and do a few power lifts to warm up all the parts!

For example *(These are in percentages of my targeted PR. So for me, 70/85 is what I based my training off of)*:

Day 1

- Snatch - 60/2, 70/2, 80/2, 85/2, and 90/1-2
- Power clean - 60/2, 65/2, (70/2)3
- CDL - 80/3, 85/3, (90/2)2, 100/2
- Back Squats - 60/10, 75/8, 85/6/, 45/15 (My knees were okay a few months ago, so I did these, but really light!)
- Press - 4x3

Day 2

- Light snatches - less than 60%
- Back Squats - (If I did the squat like above, I would drop the reps to 5/3)
- Good Mornings - 3x3
- Overhead Squats - 60/4, 65/3, (70/3)2, and 75/3

Day 3

- Snatch - (65/2)3
- Snatch pull - (100/2)3
- Overhead Squat - heavy single
- CDL with 2 halts - (88/2)3

Day 4

- Clean from the knee - 60/2, 70/2, (80/2)3, 83/2
- Jerk from Rack - 60/2, 70/2, (80/2)3
- Back Squats - 60/2, 70/2, 80/2, (85/2)3
- SDL - 70/3, (80/3)2, 90//3

Then the following week I would switch up the clean to be heavy. Every fifth workout, I would go heavy for a single in the snatch or clean and jerk. I liked this one because my knees got some rest.

Then, at the end, I would do what I call "Pretty Girls" which consisted of rotator cuff exercise with light dumbbells and stretching bands. I would do some leg lifts for my abs and lower back. If my knees were a swollen mess, I would try to do some more spinning on the bike.

Yes, it is a total drag to watch your training partner snatch more than you are clean and jerking. But if you want to train another day, you will be honest with yourself. Our motto is TRAIN SMART!

I truly believe that bad technique and bad coaching leads to injury. You must be honest with your coach about how you are feeling. If you ignore it, it will get worse!

Lately, I have had some acupuncture and deep tissue work to try to get my swelling down in my knees. I have had the synovial fluid shots in my knee as well. Usually, I do this in the summer after the Master Pan Ams. If you get these shots, training has to be light and off the blocks and power stuff for 3 weeks.

I try not to focus on my injuries, but manage it. I also try not to do stupid things too close to a meet. I like snowboarding, but come late February and early March, I give it up. You have to only train the lifts and not waste time and energy on other sports.

Ice and Advil and any warming creams are my friends. Doing rotator cuff exercises with stretching bands and light dumbbells at the end of a work out can keep the doctor away!

You have to love training and the people you train with. You have to manage your expectations of what you can accomplish, but still dream of the impossible.

I set goals for my lifting and write them down. On January 1st of this year, I wrote 70/83 and becoming a Category 2 referee, and I put it on the wall above the platform I train on. I looked at my goals every time I trained, which kept me focused and determined. But by April, I just couldn't lift on that platform anymore. I was sick of looking at it and couldn't stand the pressure anymore. I felt like I would never get there. But now it is June, and I became a Cat 2 and at Masters Nationals this year, I cleaned and jerked 83. Only one more goal to go before 2015!

Also, you need to get a coach you love and trust! My coach of 20 years, Shane Miller, has seen the best of me and the worst of me, sometimes in the same minute! He has seen me give up on myself and become determined again. He reminds me that I have grit and that I can make my goals! We always say you have to tell your coach the whole truth and nothing but the truth. You can lie to yourself, your friends and family, but never your coach.

Athlete: August Schmidt

Birth Year: 1974
Weight Class: 105 kg

- Two-time American Masters Champion
  - 2012 and 2013 Best Lifter, 35-39 age group
- National Masters Championship Silver Medalist
- 130 kg snatch (286 lbs), 155 C&J (341 lbs), 285 kg total (627 lbs) in 40-44 age group

Like many masters lifters, August Schmidt came to OLifting after a wide range of sports experiences. Although he had trained the OLifts throughout most of his athletic years, he didn't make the decision to focus on the sport exclusively until his late 30s. Currently, his best official lifts are knocking on the door of the national records in the 40-44 age group. As the owner of the massively successful East Valley CrossFit in Chandler, AZ, August also brings his experience as a coach to his own lifting pursuits. A true student of the sport, his efforts to learn have laid the groundwork for an outstanding run of masters weightlifting successes.

Interview: The most significant changes in my training have been specialization and consistency. I've competed in a lot of different sports and weightlifting has always been an important part of my training, but competing in weightlifting always took a lesser priority. I played rugby competitively from 1994-2009 with breaks here and there due to injury and life demands. In 2001, I competed in my first weightlifting meet. Since then, I trained for it and continued competing sporadically. I've trained with weightlifting as the priority off and on over the years; starting in 2013 I've pretty much trained exclusively for Weightlifting.

Initially, I learned weightlifting on my own. I studied Jim Schmitz's book and video, *Olympic Style Weightlifting for the Beginner & Intermediate Weightlifter*. Artie Drechsler's *Weightlifting Encyclopedia* was also very helpful. In 2000, I moved to San Diego to play rugby and to experience California. At that time, I looked up Coach Mike Burgener in order to get some exposure to a true weightlifting expert. On occasion, I'd make the drive up to his house for a training session. I also did the USAW Level 1 with him in 2001. That same year, Coach Burgener took me to my first meet, The California State Championships. Believe it or not, I forgot my lifting shoes and had to borrow a pair from one of his sons; I think it was Beau.

Shortly after that meet, I moved to Arizona, where I took a job as the Strength Coach at Dobson High School. While at Dobson, I started the school's weightlifting club and competed in meets a couple of times a year. In 2004, Matt Foreman moved back to Arizona and also took a job teaching at Dobson High School. Matt brought a lot to the weightlifting scene in Arizona and significantly improved my understanding of the sport in the time that we taught and coached together.

After leaving teaching to pursue opportunities in the private sector, I started training in my garage. My friend Stu Christansen had an interest in CrossFit and kept pushing me to start doing CrossFit workouts. Once he talked me into it, I saw pretty quickly that CrossFit was something special. The CrossFit business model made sense, and it gave me an opportunity to get back into the field of strength and conditioning. In 2009, I affiliated with CrossFit and started the process of building East Valley CrossFit.

The 2011 Master Nationals was my first masters meet; I competed in that meet immediately after completing the CrossFit Open. At the time, I was still training for CrossFit and wasn't specializing in weightlifting. The masters meets were a lot of fun. CrossFit training combined with my background in weightlifting allowed me to be competitive. However, to win national meets and to have a shot at setting records, I had to make the commitment to being a full-time weightlifter. So in 2013, I finally decided to dedicate my training exclusively to weightlifting.

My approach to training has varied over the years, but I've found that as a master lifter I have the most success when I train three days a week, employ three exercises per session, and plan my training based on percentages. I've found that using percentages is much more effective for me because it removes some of the ego and emotion from choosing weights. I like to change the exercise selection in each training session. What I mean by that is that a Monday training session will almost always have three exercises, but every Monday will consist of different exercises. I generally like to snatch twice a week, clean & jerk once a week (usually split), and pull two to three times a week. In addition, I'll usually push press and power clean once a week. I generally start with a competition lift or derivative, then I follow that with a pull, and then squat.

I usually take a week of rest prior to a competition and at least a week of rest afterwards. Following meets, my knees tend to be pretty irritated for up to a month. When starting a new training cycle following a meet, I've found that I have to keep the intensities low, especially in the squats. When I do start squatting again, I usually stick to 50%-60% of my 1RM until everything starts feeling good again. On the A-lifts, I usually start out with sets of 2-3 reps in the 65%-75% range. After a couple of weeks working in that range, I'll push up to 80%-85% in the A-lifts. I find that my most productive work takes place in that 80%-85% range, performing sets of 1-2 reps for a total volume of 8-12 reps. This is when I'll spend a lot of time building strength, speed and consistency. After 4-6 weeks of work in that 80%-85% range, I'll start touching 90%+ for single with a volume of 1-4 reps. At this point in the cycle, I'm usually ready to hit PRs and compete.

I generally don't do a very good job of managing my mobility and recovery work. I'm not very disciplined about stretching or icing following training. The one thing that I do very consistently to help with recovery is get massages. During periods of intensive training, I've gotten massages up to 3 times a week on a regular basis. The biggest help that I've found for pain management is ibuprofen. I generally don't take ibuprofen during training; I like to save it for immediately prior to competition. I feel like this gives it a lot more efficacy. It's been very effective for decreasing inflammation in my knees and making things work a bit more smoothly.

Train less frequently, do most of your work at lower intensities, and find a good massage therapist!

Athlete: Jim Malone

Birth Year: 1967
Weight Class: +105 kg

- American Masters Champion
- Pan American Masters Silver Medalist
- 106 kg snatch (232 lbs), 146 kg C&J (321 lbs) at 47 years old

As a strength and conditioning coach for Major League Baseball, Jim Malone brings an extensive amount of professional experience to his own career as a weightlifter. Like some of the athletes we've looked at, he came to competitive Olympic lifting at a later age. With a long background in powerlifting and general strength training, he decided to commit his focus on OLifting in recent years. Now in his 40s, Jim is setting new personal records every year and winning medals at all of the major masters championship meets. Going over 300 lbs in the C&J when you're past 45 years of age gives you automatic street cred in weightlifting, so Jim's perspective on training offers a great deal to all the aging warriors of the world.

Interview: The biggest way my training has changed is from a volume standpoint. I do much less volume than I used to do. I was raised on a combination of "Muscle & Fitness" and "Powerlifting USA" in the early 80s. I'm 47 now, started training in my basement at 12, and joined my first gym at 14. I'd read routines and try them. I latched on to a few powerlifters at the gym I trained at (where coincidentally, some "old"—meaning 40ish—Olympic lifters trained, and like a dope I gravitated to the powerlifters because they lifted more weight).

We trained 5 days a week:

- Mon – Heavy squats/legs
- Tue – Heavy bench/upper
- Wed – off
- Thur – Light squat/legs
- Fri – Light bench/upper
- Sat – Deadlift/back

We'd do 5 weeks of 5s, 3 weeks of 3s, 2 weeks of 2s, and then compete. I followed the basics of that training template, for the most part, up until and through college. Plus a TON of assistance work! I'd mix in some different routines and tweak it, based on reading and learning on my own. Terry Todd's book, back in the early 80s, was also very influential. In retrospect though, all that, along with playing football, gave me the foundation of what today would be called GPP (General Physical Preparation), at least in my opinion.

Now? Having committed to Olympic lifting, and especially at this age, I limit my volume tremendously, and have dropped nearly all of my assistance work unless it's specific to the two competition lifts (SN, C&J) and squat variations. And though there are days where I hear my ego chirping in my ear about "Start benching again! Do arms! Where did your 4.5 pack go?!" I've managed to keep it in check in the interest of this new journey.

These days, as I train and learn, I pick and choose what I need/want to work on, and will use some of Greg Everett's programming as a guideline. Fortunately, having gotten to know Greg, I'll also talk to him about some adjustments that I can make based on needs and/or limitations. I also know myself well enough at this point to make some adjustments on my own; but there are times that I like to either get the outside opinion or look for the confirmation of hearing from someone else the same thing that I might be thinking. As a strength coach myself, I very much like the idea of being coached, because then I can just go "do what I'm told." (All athletes should do what their coach tells them!!) Again, at 47, the biggest adjustment I find myself making is dropping the volume down based on how I feel, especially when it comes to multiple squat sets. I will try to go 5 days a week if I can, using a M/T/W/Th/Sat template most of the time. I'll adjust as needed.

As my training evolved into my 20s, and I was still powerlifting into my mid 20s, I altered my programming to a three day per week, two week rotation, where I started training the core lifts very heavy, and spreading out the lift variations/assistance work into other workouts. The reduced number of training days was also a necessity because I was in the early part of my coaching career and didn't have the time to train as often, so I had to economize my programming.

By now, it looked like this:

- 1st Mon – heavy bench, light shoulders & triceps
- 1st Wed – heavy squats & RDL's, light back
- 1st Fri – medium incline bench, heavy barbell should press variations, light triceps
- 2nd Mon – hang cleans, leg press, leg/back assistance
- 2nd Wed – heavy close grip benching & triceps, light shoulders
- 2nd Fri – heavy deadlifting and shrugs

I evolved to this as I started seeing guys like Ed Coan and others training each lift once a week, so I took that idea and tweaked it, partially because I saw value in the variations and segmental aspect of training those variations of the 3 lifts.

Coaching and competing became too much. I went into my last two power meets immediately before my first spring training in early 1997 and haven't done a power meet since.

In my early 30s, I became more focused on aesthetics, did more bodybuilding and volume type work, leaned up some, walked around at a more "shapely" 235 or so, still benching as heavy as I could, but backed off the heavy leg training and did more conditioning work. Don't get me wrong, I went through some "bulk up" periods, squatted and deadlifted, but it was mostly to just put size on, and see where I could take my body mass and bench press (got to 505 at age 40, in a 10 year-old single ply bench shirt). It helped in a sense, because it set me apart in MLB and gave me a presence.

Buy stock in Motrin! I'd like to say that I do "everything right" because of my job and "expertise" when it comes to pre-training prep, in order to reduce the chance of injury. But for me, it often becomes about time and necessity. While I do have a great job that allows me to train, I still have to be available for others, so there are days when I'm watching the clock. What usually suffers is the "pre" routine... but all kidding aside, I do have to do a fair amount of empty bar/40 kilo movement prep (squats, pulls, good mornings, muscle snatches and power snatches/cleans), and I use bands, hip bands, stretch bands, pull-aparts. That's my injury prevention stuff. Pain management? I just sort of deal with it, I guess. I'm reluctant to use too many NSAIDs, but will from time to time. I take my fish oils, joint formulas, try to eat foods that are touted as natural anti-inflammatory, etc. I have access to hot/cold tubs for contrast, and again, due to my job, I can get some other treatment modalities if needed depending on what our ATCs might find wrong with me (provided I suck it up and admit something's wrong and ask for a diagnosis and treatment), but I know most won't have that luxury.

When it comes to warming up, I know that Greg is big on the importance of it, and he would call me lazy, but I've trained with Mike Gray as well, and you know Mike. His idea of a warm up is putting on the "Sombra" and snatching 50/70 & 90 kilos and he's ready to roll! (His snatch is so good I almost hate him!)

Enjoy the process! And I say that not being the best at it, because although I like to train, I sometimes get too "results" oriented as opposed to enjoying the process. A good deal of that, I know, is due to my impatience, because I want to get as good as I can as fast as I can. I'm so late to this amazing sport, that is the convergence of strength & athleticism, that I'm angry at myself for not coming around to it sooner when I was young and strong and explosive! I was squatting and deadlifting over 500lbs as a 220 lb 17 year-old, so I'd love to know what I could have done back then... even at 30! Learn as much as you can, take pride in refining what you're doing, and just enjoy it. I've been very lucky that Greg reached out to me just because I ordered his first book and some posters, and then he introduced me to Mike, and now I'm meeting all these great people! Having a little success hasn't hurt me, it feeds the desire and without a doubt, the ego. But I'm just enjoying being a part of the overall process and my hope is to help shine more light onto the sport.

Athlete: Chris Dariotis

Birth Year: 1949
Weight Class: 85-94 kg

- World Masters Champion
- Pan American Masters Champion
- National Masters Champion
- National Masters Record Holder
  - Multiple national records in different age groups and weight classes
  - 102.5 kg snatch (225 lbs), 142 kg C&J (313 lbs), 94 kg bodyweight class (208 lbs), 55-59 age group
- World Masters Record Holder
  - 125 kg C&J (275 lbs), 85 kg bodyweight class (187 lbs), 60-64 age group

Chris Dariotis has one of the longest weightlifting careers of our interviewed athletes, going all the way back to 1958. After national championship success in his 20s and a long hiatus from the sport, Chris returned in the masters division to basically rewrite the record books in the various age groups he has competed in over the last 10-15 years. As a 5-time World Masters Champion, he is one of the most successful masters athletes in our country's history. A 275 lb C&J in the 60-64 age group at 187 lbs bodyweight... seriously? With numbers like that, his longevity and successful training approach speak for themselves.

Interview: My father introduced me to weight training when I was 9 years old: twice a week training sessions at the Washington Athletic Club. When I started, I could not do a chin-up or even a sit up. We taught ourselves how to perform the Olympic lifts by looking at photographs in Strength and Health magazine. No videos or even movies back then (this was 1958). The biggest lift that I saw back then was a 305 lb press by Tony Angell. One day I remember training next to Jack LaLane as he did multiple chin-ups.

Eventually my dad built an addition onto our garage and we started our own team, American Systems, named after my dad's business. We had about 20 lifters on our team including John Raffael (82.5 kg lifter who did a 140 kg snatch and 187 kg C&J), Jake Stephan, National Heavyweight Champion (155 kg snatch and 197 kg C&J), and Gary Deal (third place finish at the 1973 Pan Am Games). I became a strong teenage lifter who also competed in track and football.

I went to college in Los Angeles and began training with Bob Hise II. His son, Bob Hise III was the first person who taught me how to move under a clean instead of power cleaning. That winter was the first time that I cleaned 300 pounds while weighing 165 pounds. At the end of the school year, I travelled together with the LA YMCA team to York, PA to train in Bob Hoffman's gym in preparation to compete in the Teenage Nationals. Due to a technical issue with my entry, I was prevented from competing on the platform, but I totaled in the training room doing the following lifts: 305 lb press (equaling Tony Angell's lift, one of the highlights of my career), 245 lb snatch and 325 lb C&J, at a bodyweight of 165 lbs. Had I been on the platform, I would have beat the winner (Russ Prior, Canadian Superheavyweight Champion in later years) by 100 pounds. This brings me to my first set of rules to be a competitive weightlifter:

- You must decide and make a commitment to enter a contest.
- You must train regularly and smartly.
- You must submit your entry and verify that it has been accepted.
- You must travel to the competition.
- You must make intelligent training choices the week before the competition.
- You must show up on time and make the weigh-in.
- You must choose your opening attempts wisely and make them.

Now for masters competitors: Enjoy the competition and your fellow competitors. Life is too short to view your competitors as adversaries, there only to be beaten. When I reflect back on 50 years of weightlifting competition, I think back about the people that I have met along the way and my heart has been warmed by those that I see at masters competitions who remember me and who share in common experiences.

I had the advantage of having learned the movements at an early age and retaining some degree of flexibility. Otherwise I would advise a new lifter to learn and to practice the movements and to gradually work on increasing your flexibility. Once you have learned those basics (and I know that it can take a lifetime to learn these) by just doing the basic exercises you can develop strength at an advanced age as progressively as when you were young, with an allowance for the effects of time. My best result at age 29 was

132.5 kg snatch (292 lbs) and 167.5 C&J (369 lbs) at 82 kg bodyweight (180 lbs). Then I trained 4 times per week, 4 to 6 exercises per workout, classic lifts to 90% or 95% (I have never lifted more in training than at a competition), pulls to 105%, squats to 120% of cleans (typically for 3 reps and a few variations on weak areas). You must do your utmost to stress your muscles without incurring injuries as these will hold you back or possibly end your career. At this time, I was coached by Wes Woo, 2 time Canadian Olympic coach who had travelled to Russia in the 60s and had translated a training manual by Medvedev. When I lifted my highest weights, my coach chose them for me and I didn't even know what was on the bar.

This was the Canadian Championships in 1977. I did not train or compete again until 2001, 24 years. I had to relearn the movements and get my body to move again in the same way. I trained much the same way, however, 3-4 days a week, squats, pulls, a few lifts, and some assistance exercises. I don't really make a plan for what I want to do, but I react to how my body feels on that day, and I get a feeling of what I need to do. At the Bad Mother Open in 2002, I did 107.5 kg snatch (237 lbs) and 145.5 kg C&J (320 lbs), my highest total as a master, weighing 91 kg (200 lbs). That was 84% of my best ever total. My total has decreased each year from then by about 1% per year. Before the Bad Mother, I did the lifts more times per week, while still doing squats and pulls, but doing the lifts that many times is too hard on the joints and on the adrenal glands, so I have since backed off to few lifts during the regular training cycle, just slowly increasing them during the two months prior to a major competition.

Currently I am doing a lot of hard physical labor in my landscaping profession while training for the Masters Worlds in Copenhagen. I am very fortunate to have my wife, Margy Dariotis, as my training partner, who is focused on competing in her second Masters Worlds, otherwise I might miss more training days than I have. We try to train Monday, Wednesday and Saturday. We squat three times per week, two back and one front. Try to front squat what you want to clean for 3 reps. Do pulls for one of the lifts each workout. I don't go over 100%, otherwise it becomes a deadlift, but Margy is stronger and can go heavier. Since the contest is two months away, I try to do each lift once per week and once every 2-3 weeks to make a total on a weekend. I try to stay simple and consistent, but to put maximum effort into the heaviest lifts of the day, without failing. If I miss a snatch twice, I am done with that for that day. I can't do more than 5 or 6 clean and jerks during a workout. I never try to beat my meet PRs in training, but keep believing in the back of my mind that I will be able to do 10% more during the excitement of a contest.

So far it has worked pretty well. I have competed in 11 Master's Worlds and have won 5 golds and 5 silvers. Once I finished last because I did not follow one of my rules and bombed out in the snatch. Along the way I have accomplished 2 Masters World Records and 32 National or Pan Am Records. But, most importantly I can take pride in my accomplishments and have enjoyed getting to know so many fine people in the weightlifting world and have had many great travel experiences.

Athlete: Jo Ann Aita

Birth Year: 1970
Weight Class: 58 kg

- Pan American Masters Champion
  - Grand Master Award winner in 2014
- Pan American Masters Record Holder
  - 68 kg SN (149 lbs), 83 kg C&J (182 lbs), 151 kg total (332 lbs) at 58 kg bodyweight (127 lbs), 40-44 age group
- USA National Championship competitor

Jo Ann Aita has been putting together quite a hot streak in recent years. Although she, like some of our other contributors, didn't start weightlifting until a later age, her talent and work ethic have propelled her to the national level both as a masters competitor and also in the open division. Jo Ann has competed in the US National Championship (not just the masters division, the big-time *nationals), going head-to-head with women half her age. She has been breaking records and making outstanding improvements in her 40s, and she was able to provide some great responses to a few of our questions.*

Interview: When I started competing in weightlifting in 2004, I was already 34 years old, so I started as nearly a masters lifter. I actually started as a "hobbyist" training only 2 days per week, and I have become more and more dedicated to competitive lifting over the past 5 years. In reality, I train many more hours per week today than when I was younger. But this is primarily due to my increased interest in the sport, my change in careers (from bartending to coach, personal trainer, gym owner), and my husband's vast support of my lifting.

Generally, as a masters lifter, I do far more mobility and dedication to recovery in my 40s than in my 30s. I need more sleep, and it has also helped with my recovery and increased strength when I recently moved up a weight class. I focus far more on strength and SN/CJ variations, and do much less classic SN & CJ. I listen to my body and adjust reps and weight accordingly, instead of just "following" the program.

Max Aita, my husband, currently designs my program. I do a version of our "Max's Gym" Team Program. There is lots of volume and the focus is more on strength (lots of squats and presses) than SN and CJ. Max bases his program on ideas he has formed from his 18 years of experience in the sport, having trained under Steve Gough and Ivan Abadjiev for weightlifting and under Boris Sheiko for powerlifting.

I train 4-5 days per week. 1-2 days/week are generally light on the lifts (push press, power movements, pulls), with focus on remedial accessory work (YTL shoulder rehab, heavy DB row, ADPs). Because my schedule is flexible and my work has a sometimes unpredictable pattern, I sometimes split my training into 2 sessions (on average 1-2 times per week). This is due sometimes to my schedule, but sometimes because I am exhausted and the workload feels like too much for 1 session. My workouts are not written to be in 2 sessions, but sometimes Max and I adjust according to how my body feels.

I take FOREVER to warm up! I did so right from the start, but my stretching and mobilization has increased dramatically as I've gotten older and since my 2 shoulder surgeries in 2010. (FYI: by Nationals 2012, I had surpassed my pre-surgery numbers). From 34-39 years of age, my warmup lasted 20-30 minutes. Today, I average 45-60 minutes. Included with stretches and "rolling out," I also do an additional 15 minutes of "activation" work; making sure my adductors, hamstrings, lats, etc. are firing before I start lifting.

Max and I choose my exercises according to what I need. For example, in the past I did C&J nearly every training day. As a lifter, since my shoulder surgeries, my clean has grown to be about 10kg higher than my jerk. Therefore, I feel like I am losing 10kg+ on my total. In order to address this, on most cycles of my program now, I only clean 1-2 times/week, but I do some type of jerk, press, or push press 4-5 times/week. More generally, on a daily basis, my exercises include some type of pull, squat, snatch or clean and jerk, and press. I usually do SN and CJ exercises on separate days. This was not the case until this year.

I wasn't lifting in my 20s, but in my 30s, as I mentioned before, I was more of a hobbyist. When I first started, I strictly did Jim Schmitz' programming (from The Sports Palace). Jim is an excellent coach, I believe the most accomplished US coach in history. He is currently my competition coach, and continues to advise me periodically on my program (I send him Max's program, so he can keep up on what I'm doing), and helps me with injury prevention and overtraining advice. Generally, Jim's program was more conservative than my current training, and he would probably say "smarter" as far as getting less beat up, risking less injury, and becoming overtrained. I do get pretty exhausted with my current program, but I listen to my body and often reduce intensity or some of the volume, accordingly. Max and I are working on adjusting my cycles so I have an extra light week every 4-6 weeks, so I might recover better, make more progress, and lessen the risk of injury.

From 2009-2011 (39-41 years of age), I was going to maximum in the lifts far more than before or after that time, usually 3 times/week. I trained a total of 6 days/week, usually doing maximum powers on the "light" days. I was doing very little accessory work and overall strength building. In 2010, I had torn the labrum in both of my shoulders, which I ended up having surgically repaired. In hindsight, I believe that type of training, with my body, my age, and my level of technique led to my labrum tears. In 10 years of weightlifting, that is the only serious injury I have incurred.

Athlete: Jim Storch

Birth Year: 1966

Weight Class: 105 kg

- National Masters Champion
- American Masters Champion
- National Masters Record Holder
  - Multiple national records in different age groups and weight classes
  - 126 kg snatch (277 lbs), 162 kg C&J (357 lbs), 287 kg total (632 lbs), 105 kg bodyweight class (231 lbs), 45-49 age group
- American Open competitor

Jim Storch has built an extremely successful career in the masters division. At the time of this book's publication, he holds five American Masters Records across two different age groups. Still clean and jerking over 350 lbs in his late 40s, he's an ageless wonder. His training background goes back several years, but he has managed to put together his finest results in the elder phase of his weightlifting journey. With no plans to quit or retreat, Jim continues to plow forward and hoist barbells that few men his age have ever lifted.

Interview: The biggest change has been in attitude. I can still do just about any single training session I've ever been able to do in the past. The difference is, now it takes longer before I recover enough to repeat that feat. I have fun training and as soon as I notice I'm not having fun, I know it is time to change and/or walk away from what I am doing.

In the beginning of this journey (35+ years ago), my workouts were more along the lines of "bodybuilding" type workouts (often the "old" HIT one-set-to-failure in each exercise/body part workouts) with C&Js added in (because that was all that I knew of). More recently, I've been doing workouts that are inspired and modified by my understanding of the LSUS (LSU-Shreveport) workouts. In between there (once I learned of it), I used linear periodization and then non-linear periodization.

Usually, I train between 3 to 8 times per week. The warm up varies; sometimes I go through a series of light callisthenic exercises (i.e. jumping jacks, sit ups, pushups, etc.). Other times, I will just use the bar for multiple sets of squats, snatches, cleans, jerks, etc. and still other times I will row 500 or 1000 meters on a concept 2 rower. I've even just done a set of 20 or 30 wall balls or burpees. Most often, I do some mix of all of the above. I try to include some "pre-hab" stuff whether I "need" it or not.

Exercise selection is based on intent and need. I snatch, clean, jerk, squat (front, back, and overhead), curl, flip tires, throw tires, run, row, etc. What I mean by intent and need is... for example, if I plan to do a powerlifting meet and wish to prioritize it, I'll do low bar squats and such. I do NOT do low bar squats for my Olympic weightlifting (they have a negative impact on my snatch and C&J).

Sorry to be vague, but in my 20s and 30s I trained HARD and not always smart. Now I train hard and SMART (which means, among other things, that sometimes I do NOT train hard at all).

I take a break EVERYTIME I need to for whatever reason I need to. I can now walk away from a workout and only feel slightly (if at all) bad about it. I do "pre-hab" exercises for my shoulders, knees, back, anything else that needs it. I pay attention to how my body feels. I've realized that I hurt if I do nothing and I hurt if I do "everything," so I avoid both extremes and if I have to choose, I find that it is better to do something rather than nothing. I use Ibuprofen, etc. only as a last resort. I ice, but only for ten minutes at a time. I stretch... as much (maybe more) to relax as for flexibility.

Be patient, have fun, enjoy life and lifting. As a master... why the hell would anyone want to do this if it's not fun?

Summary/Analysis of Athlete Interviews:

That's ten interviews from highly successful masters weightlifters. As you saw, we have a very diverse cross-section of experiences here. Some of these athletes began their lifting careers when they were young, and then continued into their older years. Others didn't get into the game until they were already in their 30s. In other words, their journeys are probably very similar to those of you who are reading this thing. They come from all walks of life, just like you.

I want to make some comments and observations about what they shared. We got a terrific amount of training input from them, but it might be a little confusing to some of you simply because of the diversity in their methods. Let's list some thoughts and see if we can tie a few things together:

Different approaches = common results: Once again, we see one of the fundamental concepts in OLifting. These people don't all train the same way. They use different volume, different intensity, different exercises, different frequency, etc. However, every one of them has been successful. That's probably the biggest piece of learning you need to walk away with. There's more than one way to skin a cat, period. If anybody ever tells you any different, that person doesn't know jack squat about weightlifting.

Training methodology is dependent on personal circumstances: Fred Lowe's training program works for Fred Lowe. We know this is true because Fred Lowe gets great results from it. Fred Lowe's training program might not work for Matt Foreman, or Jodi Stumbo, or you. One of the things that's so interesting about these masters is that they've found productive ways to modify, adapt, improvise, and invent. Once you get older, many of the generally accepted rules of weightlifting go out the window. You have to figure out what's going to make YOU successful, and it'll be completely dependent on your own intuition, experimentation, and results.

A "workout" doesn't necessarily have to include lifting heavy weights: When an athlete says he trains six times per week, that doesn't guarantee that he's doing heavy SN, C&J, or squats in every one of those workouts. Some of those training sessions might be extremely light technique work. Some of them might not even include a barbell. They might be nothing but abdominal work, dumbbell exercises for arms or shoulders, flipping tires or running (as Jim Storch mentioned), or several other modes of exercise. You need to remember that a "workout" can mean many things. It might mean heavy OLifts, or it might mean something else that will make you stronger and healthier.

We're all still in the development process: Even people who have won world championships are still looking for the perfect training strategy. Just because you've broken an American record doesn't ensure you're doing everything exactly perfectly. I've had a lot of experience and success, and I can personally guarantee that I'm still searching for all the right angles on my program. Obviously I've found some strategies that work really well, but there's always the knowledge that nobody is flawless and everything can be improved. If you read something in one of these interviews that sounds like it might not be an ideal strategy, you might be right. None of us have found the perfect Holy Grail of training programs, even if we've done big things.

It's okay for you to be a critic: You can make judgments on what these athletes are doing. There's nothing wrong with that. You might read Mike Gray's training interview and you say to yourself, "Mike is doing some things wrong. He would probably be more successful if he made some changes." That doesn't make you a jagoff. It just means you're thinking creatively and using your brain. Now if you get on the internet and start talking smack about Mike Gray's training program, THAT makes you a jagoff. Running your mouth on the internet is pathetic. It can also be dangerous because you might bump into that person someday. If you've ever seen Mike Gray, you'd know what I mean when I say "dangerous." But I digress...The point I'm making is that there's nothing wrong with speculating about ways to improve things, as long as you handle your speculation the right way.

Lighter athletes and women generally recover faster than heavier male athletes: I've been noticing this throughout my whole career. When I was training with the Calpians back in the 90s, we had some female lifters and lighter men (85 kg and below) who could handle freaky volume. They could train all the time and take lots of heavy attempts, and their bodies would respond really well. It's just not like that with the big puppies. Heavyweight lifters require more recovery time, plain and simple. When I started lifting in my teens, I weighed around 88 kilos (193 lbs). Over the years, I gradually grew up to 127 kilos (280 lbs). Brothers and sisters, there's a huge difference in what your body feels like at 88 kilos compared to 127 kilos. When I was lighter, I could handle tons of volume and my recovery was instantaneous. It's just not like that when you're a superheavyweight. Heavy training takes longer to recover from, plain and simple.

Don't just look at the WHAT, look at the WHY: When you read the information from these experts, don't confine yourself to simply examining their training programs. Look at the reasons WHY they train the way they do. Some of them base their programs on past injuries, individual goals, or specific limitations from their bodies. Some of their programs revolve around jobs or family commitments. Ask yourself if your personal circumstances are similar to theirs, or completely different. It doesn't make much sense to copy somebody's training program if your life requirements are totally dissimilar to theirs.

My sincere appreciation goes out to all the great lifters who contributed to this book. There's nothing better than learning from the best. Their ideas can make us all better, and I'm grateful to them for pitching in to help the upcoming generations of masters weightlifters.

Programming Phase Six: Sample Training Programs

Obviously, we've reached a point where you've had a lot of input from different individuals. Some of the athletes we interviewed outlined their training in detail, and some used more general descriptions.

What I want to do now is simply offer you a wide range of training programs that could potentially be used by a master lifter. Since we've clearly established the idea that limiting volume and backing off is crucial in your older years, I'm going to show you some two- and three-day-per-week programs. Some of these will incorporate the principles you read about in our athlete interviews. Some will be actual programs that have been used by masters lifters I know who weren't featured in the interview section. The main idea is that you, as an older lifter, are looking for training ideas that will make you productive at your age, and you might be in a position where you're only capable of two or three good training days per week.

I understand that it's not impossible for an older lifter to train hard five times per week. There are some people who can still handle large amounts of work in their older years. They're very rare, but they do exist. Those people have plenty of resources available to them because there's no shortage of five day (or more) programs floating around out there. We've already looked at two of the ones I personally used with the Calpian club when we were in the Programming Phase Four section. However, many of you can't keep up with that much volume anymore. Hey, don't feel bad. I can't do it either. That's why you need some organized plans that will give you a shot to train productively without walking around in screaming agony all the time. Here are some potential plans you could follow.

PROGRAM 1

Monday

- Snatch
- Rack Jerk
- Front Squat
- Ab work

Wednesday

- Clean
- Snatch Pulls (alternate each week with clean pulls)
- Back Squat
- Ab work

Friday

- Snatch
- C&J

- RDLs
- Ab work

NOTES: In this program, the main competition lifts are basically being worked twice a week, which is a solid amount of focus. The snatch is being trained twice; the C&J is being trained once and then broken up into its components (Rack Jerk, Clean) on other days. There are two squat workouts per week, which is often plenty for an older lifter. There are also three different pulling movements (snatch pulls, clean pulls, RDLs) on the program. This would be a substantial amount of work for a masters lifter. Athletes in their 30s or 40s would be good candidates for this program. Athletes in their 50s or 60s could also give it a try, but with caution.

PROGRAM 2

Tuesday

- Snatch
- C&J
- Clean Pulls
- Ab work

Thursday

- Push Press
- Snatch Pulls
- Back Squat
- Ab work

Saturday

- Snatch
- C&J
- Front Squat
- Ab work

NOTES: Once again, we have a three-day program. Here we keep the competition movements together on the same days twice per week (SN/C&J on Tuesday and Saturday), so the important stuff is covered. The Thursday workout will be somewhat easier (just pulls and squats), which is deliberate because it allows some recovery. There are still two squat workouts per week, along with pulls being used twice. This is very similar to program #1, and the same athletes (30s or 40s) would probably have the most success with it. This program allows the athlete to train the competition lifts (SN/C&J) in "meet circumstances" by always doing them on the same day. This can be a great asset for a competitive lifter because doing both lifts at a meet won't be a shock to the system, since they're trained together on a regular basis. It would be strongly advised to make one of these SN/C&J workouts heavy each week, with the other one being much lighter. It's basically just the old "heavy day/light day" principle.

PROGRAM 3

Monday

- Power Snatch
- Snatch-grip Deadlift
- Ab work

Wednesday

- Power Clean & Power Jerk
- Front Squat
- Ab work

Friday

- Snatch
- C&J
- Back Squat
- Ab work

NOTES: This is another three-day program, but the overall approach is much different. The full competition movements are only being performed once a week (Friday) and the other two days use only power movements. This program might be a good choice for a lifter who needs more recovery time after doing the full SN and C&J. Friday is obviously the toughest day because A) it's the only day when SN/C&J are trained, and B) it's the only day that has three lifting exercises. That's why Friday is always followed by two rest days before resuming training on Monday. Also, Monday and Wednesday are mostly power movements, where the lifts are obviously received at an "above parallel" position. This gives the athlete a break from the pounding of hitting that deep bottom position all the time. Athletes who are getting into their older years and can't hit the full lifts as often might want to give this a try.

PROGRAM 4

Tuesday

- Snatch
- RDLs
- Ab work

Thursday

- Rack Jerk
- Power Clean
- Ab work

Saturday

- C&J
- Front Squat (alternate each week with back squat)
- Ab work

NOTES: This program includes only one squat workout per week. This would be useful for older lifters who can handle three days of training per week, but simply can't handle a lot of squatting. The competition lifts and some variant work are incorporated, but only one squat day. This would be a last-resort type situation, because continuing to squat twice a week should be a primary goal for any lifter.

PROGRAM 5

Monday

- Push Press
- Clean-grip Deadlift
- Front Squat
- Ab work

Friday

- Snatch
- C&J
- Back Squat
- Ab work

NOTES: With this program, the first training day of the week has almost no highly explosive movements. All three exercises are relatively low-impact, mainly focusing on basic strength. Impact on the joints is limited. The second workout of the week features the hardest work. This program, quite frankly, would be a good choice for lifters who only have one really hard day per week in them. It might not look like much on paper, but a program like this could lead to tremendous success for an older lifter because, like program #4, it carries very little risk of overtraining. Some people's bodies get banged up much quicker than others, for a variety of reasons. The athlete is almost guaranteed to feel good on most training days because of the limited workout frequency, and training will almost always be more productive when the athlete feels fresh and rested. Two days per week doesn't sound like enough, but you've obviously already heard from some top masters lifters who train this way.

PROGRAM 6

Tuesday

- Snatch
- Back Squat
- Ab work

Friday

- C&J
- Front Squat
- Ab work

NOTES: Remember the coaches I talked about in the beginning of this book? You know, the ones who want to train Olympians and don't have much knowledge or interest in working with older lifters? Those coaches would probably laugh at this program. There's nothing scientific about it, and it's not a lot of work. But THAT'S THE WHOLE POINT. Let's say you're getting older and you're starting to doubt whether you'll be able to continue OLifting. You're beat up all the time and it looks like you should probably call it quits and take up golf or something. This is a major bummer in your life because you desperately still want to be a lifter. You get depressed when you think about quitting. Okay, what if THIS program was the magic formula that kept you in the sport? What if you gave this a try and found out that it allowed you to stay competitive? And here's a crazy thought... what if you continued to lift good weights without feeling destroyed all the time? If that happens, and you get to continue doing what you love, is this program still a stupid joke? No, brothers and sisters, it isn't. Listen, you have to remember that the opinions of a bunch of young athletes and coaches don't matter to you. They haven't been where you've been (yet) and they don't know how you feel. If you use a program like this, and they laugh at it, screw them. You might travel to the National Masters Championship every year and win medals until you're 75 with a program like this. That would be a pretty good way to grow old, don't you agree?

The basic rule of programming: As we've said repeatedly, there are many ways to design a training program that works for you. The ones you just saw were suggestions that might fit an older lifter who has limited (in some cases, VERY limited) ability to train, either because of physical status or job demands. The "anything at all is better than nothing at all" principle is the overriding guide to the whole thing. If you want to use one of these exact programs, go ahead. If you want to combine some ideas from various ones, that's fine too. The only factor that makes your program good or bad is its effectiveness. If it works, it's the right program. That's a plain-vanilla mentality, but that's how you have to think when you're a weightlifter with a large accumulation of birthdays.

NOTE: I want to make it clear that these programs could definitely be supplemented with additional workouts during the week where there is no barbell work, just pre-hab, stretching, core work, etc. Look at Program 5, which was:

Monday

- Push Press
- Clean-grip Deadlift

- Front Squat
- Ab work

Friday

- Snatch
- C&J
- Back Squat
- Ab work

It would be entirely possible to follow this program, but also add a few more workouts during the week that don't involve heavy lifting. Let's say you wanted to try this routine, where the workouts happen on Monday and Friday, but add some sessions on Wednesday and Saturday where you work with bands, kettlebells, dumbbells, or maybe some cardio work. Then it becomes a four-day program, but only two of those days are lifting-centered. If it works, great! As we've said, there are no rules for any of this. You can tinker with these programs and make as many individual adjustments as you want. Then there's an easy way to find out if it's going to be successful...just try it.

Acknowledgment of the Genetic Exceptions

At this point, I think there's something important we need to mention. Obviously, most of the training discussion we've done so far has been based on the idea of reducing volume, frequency, intensity, etc. as you get older. The general undertone has been that you'll have to train less and back off more when you progress into your masters years. I think this idea will apply to many of you, and you'll probably benefit greatly if you take it seriously. However, we do need to recognize the fact that there are some genetic freaks walking among us. These are people who simply don't age the same as everybody else. When they're 48, they still look and feel like they're 28. You've seen people like this, right? With these individuals, it's entirely possible that they might not have to back off their training as much as the rest of us.

If a masters athlete has a lot of natural genetic blessings, he/she might be able to handle a training program that's built for a young person. I think situations like this are rare, but they're not totally unheard of. Because of this, we need to concede the point that some of you might not HAVE to back off your training as much as I'm describing. You might be one of those freaks. I suppose the only way to know for sure is to give it a whirl. If you put yourself on a training program like the first one I outlined, a five-day hardcore program that has been designed specifically for young full-time Olympic hopefuls in their teens and early 20s, you'll probably get some pretty clear signals that tell you if it's suitable. If you're physically destroyed in a month and you can barely walk up a flight of stairs because your knees and back are so hammered, that's your body telling you that the program is too much. On the other hand, if you make tons of progress and start hitting new personal records without any injuries or substantial pain, I guess the program works for you. I'll be totally honest, I've been a weightlifter for a very long time and I haven't seen many of these cats... the ones who defy the laws of nature. I've seen plenty of people who THINK they can do it, and they usually find out the hard way that they're human just like the rest of us. Regardless, I don't want to continue our analysis of masters lifting without accepting the possibility that some people will still be able to do the same things at 40 that they did at 20. It's a crazy world we live in.

We're going to transition back into the programming study, and the book will continue to operate under the general understanding that masters athletes will have to train with less demanding programs than young athletes. Still, let's always keep it in the back of our minds that this rule isn't set in stone. If you're one of those genetic wonders, you can thank God for it and train as hard as you want. But you should still heed the advice of this book, because you're not gonna get away with it forever. Your genetic freakiness will dry up, someday. Unfortunately, that's a promise.

Programming Phase Seven: Weekly Loading and Weight Selection

We've talked a lot about feeling physically beat up, right? Half of our discussions have revolved around how fatigued and achy you can get when you're a masters lifter. The important idea to remember here is that your physical status is going to be mainly determined by how heavy you're going in training. We've talked about training only two or three times a week to avoid injury and damage, right? Listen, you could train six days a week as a master if the weights you lift in those six days are light enough. If you wanted to confine yourself to constantly working with tiny weights that will have almost no chance of beating you up, you could train all the time. However, you're smart enough to understand that you're not really going to make any progress unless you push your limits somewhat. That means you need to have some heavy weights in there somewhere. That brings us to the big question: how heavy should we go, and how often?

I actually taught a seminar about this exact topic not long ago, so I'm going to include some of my notes here.

QUESTION: *Once I have a weekly program established, how heavy am I supposed to go in each workout?*

As with most topics in weightlifting, there's more than one way to approach the subject of weight selection (loading) in a training program. Various methods are used by coaches and athletes around the world, and many of them result in successful weightlifting performance. In this section, we'll be analyzing three different loading strategies.

METHOD 1: PERCENTAGE-BASED LOADING

This is a training approach where the athlete's daily loading is planned and pre-determined using various percentages of the athlete's 1RM (one-rep max). There are multiple ways to set up a percentage loading schedule. One of them is a simple weekly progression from the lightest percentages at the beginning of the program to the heaviest ones at the end. Here are two examples of what this would look like:

17-week Progressive Training Cycle: Percentage-Based

This cycle would lead to a competition at the end of the 17th week. Percentages are simply set up to increase incrementally from week one through week 15, with weeks 16-17 using lower percentages to allow the athlete to "taper" for the competition. Tapering is a practice that reduces the heavy loading immediately prior to a contest, allowing the athlete to gain rest and recovery.

- The percentages are according to the athlete's highest record weight in a specific exercise. So if an athlete has a top snatch of 140 kilos, 78% would be 109 kilos (140 x .78 = 109.2)
- This particular program also uses a deloading week every 4th week. This is basically just a light week that allows the athlete to recovery and avoid overtraining.

Program:
Week 1 - 70%
Week 2 - 73%
Week 3 - 75%
Week 4 - 60 % (deloading week)
Week 5 - 78%
Week 6 - 80%
Week 7 - 83%
Week 8 - 60% (deloading week)
Week 9 - 85%
Week 10 - 88%
Week 11 - 90%
Week 12 - 60% (deloading week)
Week 13 - 93%
Week 14 - 95%
Week 15 - 98%
Week 16 - 90% (taper week)
Week 17 - Meet Week (Monday - 85%, Wednesday - 60%, Saturday - compete)

Obviously, no exercises were specified here. This layout is simply a basic example to show you what a progressive percentage-based program looks like on paper. If you decide to use this training method, you can manipulate it any way you choose to get the results you're looking for within your own time frame.

When the program says "Week 6 80%" that might mean the athlete goes to 80% in the snatch on one training day during week 6, and then goes to 80% in C&J on a different day (depending on how the weekly program is organized). Lifting the specified percentage for both SN and C&J in the same workout should be approached with caution, because that will eventually lead to lifting 95% or 98% in both competition lifts during the same workout in the final weeks of the program. This is a lot of work for one day and could increase the chance for overtraining.

5-week Block Cycle: Percentage-Based

This is a different type of loading schedule where the athlete is basically using 5-week (or possibly longer) mini cycles to build up maximum weights. This system plans for the athlete to attempt 100% weights once a month, with the heaviest week always being followed by a deloading week. It's important to know that "100%" means the top lifts the athlete is capable of during that particular week. If the athlete is in a perfect performance state and ready to attempt all-time personal records, that's great. If "100%" in that particular week leaves the athlete hitting 4-5 kilos below personal records, that's fine too. The point is that each mini-cycle gives the athlete a chance to go heavy at the end, with the understanding that "heavy" is relative to that particular time.

Program:
Week 1 - 83%
Week 2 - 87%
Week 3 - 92%
Week 4 - Work to maximum (100%, possibly attempt new records)
Week 5 - Recovery week - 60% or complete rest, depending on physical state

If week 5 was complete rest, spending one or two weeks afterwards working back up using 75-80% might be sensible prior to hitting the upcoming 84-89-94% weeks. This would obviously change the weekly pace of the program (making the next mini-cycle 6-7 weeks long instead of 5), but it might be necessary and beneficial to do this.

Week 6 - 84%
Week 7 - 89%
Week 8 - 94%
Week 9 - Work to maximum (100%, possibly attempt new records)
Week 10 - Recovery week - 60% or complete rest, depending on physical state

Once again, this is just a sample layout to help you understand the basic structure of block percentage programming. As with the 17-week progressive program, you could manipulate it in a variety of ways to fit your plans and goals. I've used similar looking cycles to this over the years, obviously with modifications and adjustments.

There's good and bad in everything, so let's look at some potential advantages and drawbacks of this programming style.

Positives of percentage-based training

- It's easy for athletes to follow.

- There's no daily guesswork with weights.
- Percentages can be structured to avoid overtraining and "peak" athletes for specific times.

Areas for concern with percentage-based training

- It assumes that athletes will feel good on specific days.
  - Multiple variables determine the athlete's daily performance state (level of soreness, fatigue, arousal, etc.). You never have a guarantee that you're going to be ready for big lifts on a given day.
  - If a heavy percentage is planned on a day when the athlete is in a low performance state, the plan can be skewed.
    - Example: There's one specific day when the athlete is supposed to attempt 95%, but that weight can't be lifted because of low performance state. The athlete only makes it to 85% that day, and another shot at 95% might not be planned at an optimal time.
- Potential for missing "strike while the iron is hot" moments
  - If an athlete feels great (high performance state) on a day when only 80% weights are programmed, an opportunity for a new personal record might be missed.

METHOD 2: LINEAR PROGRESSION LOADING

This is a training method where the athlete's weights are pre-planned, but not according to percentages. A coach selects a target weight that the athlete is supposed to lift on a specific day (such as a competition), and then "works backwards" week-to-week to the beginning of the cycle.

I've already given you one example of linear progression loading when we looked at my own personal training program for the 2008 American Masters Championship earlier in Programming Phase Four. I'll show you another example here, once again using one of my own routines.

Sample Program:
Matt Foreman, 2012 American Masters Championships

This is an 18-week program I followed while training for the 2012 American Masters. There are several factors to mention with this program:

- I was 40 years old at this time and I trained twice a week (Tuesday and Saturday).
- The only lifts I put on the program were SN, C&J, and BSQ because these were the only ones that needed a loading plan.
- Only top weights of the day are listed, no warm-ups. Everything is in kilos.
- I was doing no front squats at all during this time. They caused too much wear and tear on my body and I was able to get all the leg strength I needed from back squats.
- Weights are listed as SN/C&J/BSQ. So, when looking at the program, something like 90/110/140 means the workout was:
  - Work up to a 90 kilo SN for at least a single, maybe two or three singles.
  - Work up to a 110 kilo C&J, same manner as the snatch.
  - Work up to 140 kilos in the BSQ. On this particular program, I let my daily physical condition determine the number of reps I did with my top squat weights for the week. If I had a weight like 140 listed for that week and I felt fine, I would do the 140 for a set of three reps, possibly two sets of three. If I was feeling banged up, I might just hit the 140 for a single and be done with it. But sets of three reps (triples) were the highest I went.
  - Remaining assistance work, like RDLs and core work, isn't included with this loading progression.
- I planned deloading into the program every four weeks to allow more recovery and avoid overtraining.
- I had ACL reconstruction surgery on my knee in the summer of 2011. ACL surgeries, as you might know, are very difficult and require several months of recovery. After the surgery, I made the decision to make a very slow comeback. I wanted to make sure I didn't rush anything, and I was fine with the idea of easing back into competition with relatively smaller weights. I was also 40 years old at this point, which led me to err on the side of caution even more. By the summer of 2012, my knee was feeling back to normal and I was ready to aim for a 120 kg snatch and 140 C&J at this particular competition.
- Prior to starting this program, the biggest weights I had lifted in my comeback from the ACL surgery were: SN - 115 kg, C&J - 137 kg, Total - 252 kg

- These weights were very easy, but I still decided to progress along steadily instead of rushing anything. I felt like the chance of re-injuring myself would be increased if I went nuts and attacked some 10-15 kilo increases too soon, so I held back to stay safe.
- I used a very slow, gradual weekly build-up on this program. At this point in my career, I really only felt like I needed to hit 90% or above three or four times prior to competition.
- For the first 11 weeks of the program, I would hit my highest weekly target weights in the same workout because they were light enough to avoid any risk of overtraining. In other words, my target SN and C&J weights for the week could be done on the same day. Therefore, my training week for Week 9, for example, would look like this (target weights for this week were 103 in SN and 122 in C&J, 185 in BSQ):
  - Tuesday (light day): SN up to 90 kg for 3 singles, C&J up to 110 for 2 singles, BSQ up to 185x3 (target squat weight for that week), abdominal work and stretching to finish the workout.
  - Saturday (heavy day): SN up to 103 for 1-2 singles, C&J up to 122 for 1-2 singles, BSQ up to 165-175x3 (lighter squat day), abdominal work and stretching to finish the workout.
- During the two weeks when I hit the heaviest weights of the program (13 and 14), I alternated light SN/heavy C&J one week, and then heavy SN/light C&J the following week. This was done to avoid overtraining.
- I planned my heaviest weights of the program to be 4-5 weeks away from the competition. This seems very early, but I really wanted to make sure I had complete recovery in the last few weeks prior to competing.

18-week loading program:

	Target SN/C&J/BSQ weights:
Week 1 -	55/75/110
Week 2 -	65/85/140
Week 3 -	75/95/160
Week 4 -	**Deload**
Week 5 -	85/105/170

Week 6 -	93/112/175
Week 7 -	98/117/180
Week 8 -	**Deload**
Week 9 -	103/122/185
Week 10 -	108/127/188
Week 11 -	113/131/192
Week 12 -	**Deload**
Week 13 -	105/136/180
Week 14 -	118/122/185
Week 15 -	**Deload**
Week 16-	95/115/180
Week 17 -	80/100/175
Week 18 -	Meet Week

Meet, 2012 American Masters Championship, Monrovia, CA

SNATCH	CLEAN & JERK
1st attempt: 110	1st attempt: 130
2nd attempt: 115	2nd attempt: 135
3rd attempt: 120	3rd attempt: 140

TOTAL: 260

Additional training notes:

- My attempts at the competition felt easy. I probably could have made 125/145, but I was glad I followed the plan.
- This entire experience was much more cautious and reserved than I was used to. My competitive career had been based on "going for broke" at meets. But an ACL surgery changes your perspective on things. After getting it done and going through the physical therapy, I was grateful just to be lifting weights again. Putting up huge totals in competition, as strange as it sounds, wasn't my top priority. Lifting successfully, having fun and staying healthy were much more important at the time. I had spent twenty years flirting with disaster, and now I wanted to take a more reserved approach.

Positives and negatives of linear progression training

These are almost exactly the same as percentage-based training. Another positive of this style is that numbers can be planned exactly. Instead of writing "88%" on a program, you can simply write "137 kg." Some athletes (myself included) like seeing exact numbers on their program, simply because it feels more precise. Since I've now given you two examples of my own training programs using linear progression planning, you can probably guess that I prefer this style. I've used it throughout the vast majority of my career.

METHOD 3: DAILY MAXIMUM LOADING

This method is substantially different from the previous two. Here, there are no weights programmed into the training plan. Once a weekly training structure has been established, along with an established plan of sets and repetitions, the athletes simply work up to the top weight they're capable of lifting each day.

In other words, we would first establish the weekly program. For example, let's say we designed a program that looked like this:

Tuesday

- Snatch - 2x3, 4x2, 3x1
- C&J - 1x2, 6x1
- Clean Pulls - 4x3 (5-10 kg above top C&J weight of the day)
- Ab work

Thursday

- Push Press - 5x3
- Snatch Pulls - 4x3 (5-10 kg above top SN weight from Tuesday)
- Back Squat - 5x5
- Ab work

Saturday

- Snatch - 3x3, 5x2
- C&J - 3x3, 5x2
- Front Squat - 2x3, 4x2
- Ab work

As you can see, the exercises are pre-planned, along with the number of sets and repetitions. I list them as set x reps, so 2x3 means two sets of three repetitions. 3x1 means three singles, etc.

With a program like this, the athlete would basically just follow the set/rep scheme, progressing up in weight throughout each set until the final sets, which would be the heaviest weights of the day. The top weight the athlete lifts is completely determined by how he/she feels that day.

For example, let's say we have a male athlete whose top snatch is 100 kg and he was following this rep scheme: Snatch - 2x3, 4x2, 3x1. The first set of the day would obviously be the lightest weight the athlete normally warms up with in a basic snatch workout, probably around 40-50 kilos. From there, the athlete would make incremental increases on each set. So the 2x3, 4x2 portion of the workout would probably look like this (on a good day): 50x3, 60x3, 70x2, 75x2, 80x2, 85x2.

At this point, the athlete can determine his physical status for that day. If he feels good, he might jump to 90 for his first single. If 90 is easy, 95 might be the next weight. If he fails at 95, he would probably repeat at the same weight, which would be his final snatch of the workout. At this point, the workout looked like this: 50x3, 60x3, 70x2, 75x2, 80x2, 85x2, 90x1, 95 (fail), 95x1.

If the athlete made 90 and 95, he might take a shot at 100 to equal his personal record. If he makes the 100, obviously he can use his best judgment at that point. If he wants to take an additional attempt at 102 for a new record, great. Or, if the 100 was difficult, he could stop there, making the workout look like this: 50x3, 60x3, 70x2, 75x2, 80x2, 85x2, 90x1, 95x1, 100x1 (possible extra attempt at 102). This would be an example of a workout when the athlete is in a high performance state.

Let's look at another example where the athlete was in a low performance state (fatigued, sore, slow, etc.). In this case, the workout might look like this: 50x3, 60x3, 70x2, 75x2, 80x2, 83x2, 86x1, 86x1, 86x1. Here, the athlete simply decided to work up to a lighter top weight because he knew he wasn't ready for any maximum attempts that day.

The point is that the athlete's judgment and daily performance state is the determinant for the weights of the workout. To state it very simply, the athlete goes for heavy weights when he feels good, and he stays with moderate weights when he feels bad.

NOTE: The title of this method (Daily Maximum Loading) makes it sound like the athlete is supposed to "max out" every day (approach 100%). Maxing out every day as a masters lifter sounds like a quick ticket to the hospital. Hopefully, the examples we just looked at make it clear that this type of programming isn't intended to do that. It's not a "go up to 100% every day" program. The athletes use their daily condition as the guide for their workouts. They probably won't feel ready to attempt new record weights on most days, and that's fine. This is a "strike when the iron is hot" method that saves the heaviest days for the times when the athlete feels best, while also acknowledging that the weights have to be held back on days when it's clearly not in the cards.

Positives of daily maximum loading

- It allows athletes and coaches some flexibility.
- It gives the athletes the opportunity to go heavy when it's appropriate, and also to back off when necessary.
- It's easier to program because there isn't much advance planning involved.

Areas for concern with daily maximum loading

- There's a temptation to go heavy too often. This is a very legitimate point with this style of training. Athletes and coaches with poor judgment and low self-control should probably avoid using this method. People like that can easily get sucked into maxing out every day, which will last a very short time before injury occurs with masters athletes.
- There's no peaking strategy involved. If an athlete uses this method to prepare for competition, it's hard to prepare reliably for top physical state at the meet.
- It's just too vague and fuzzy for some people. Individuals who like structure and precision planning might have a difficult time with this method. It doesn't appear to be based on any scientific approach. It's more of a fly-by-the-seat-of-your-pants methodology. Sometimes that comes across as being foolish; however, I've occasionally used this style of training both as an athlete and a coach. It's a little on the risky side and there's a lot of potential for mistakes if it's not blended with intelligence and self-discipline, but it is possible to train effectively with this method. I've done it, and I know other successful lifters who have as well. I don't widely recommend it, but I also won't completely dismiss it and throw it on the scrap heap.

Conclusion of Weekly Program Structure and Loading

At this point, you've seen several different training methods. If you want to construct a program that works best for you, you'll probably have to combine ideas and strategies until you find an effective plan. As I said in the beginning, masters athletes have to be innovators. You, as the athlete, are the only one who understands the exact details of your job schedule, your physical status, and your goals in weightlifting. That means your program will have to be tailored to your exact specifications. If you're in a situation where you've got a coach who can do this for you, it's terrific. However, I know several masters athletes who are being trained by young coaches who simply don't understand what it's like to be a weightlifter when you're older. Most of them are doing too much work, and their bodies are usually beat to hell. You can't be afraid to think for yourself when you're an older lifter, and you certainly can't be afraid to make changes to your program that will keep you healthy and productive. Use the information I've given you, along with the excellent words of the elite older athletes we interviewed, to find your own perfect combination.

Programming Phase Eight: Post-Workout Stretching

Now you've put together a perfect program and trained your ass off. So the workout for the day is over, you've put your weights away and taken your shoes off. Now it's just time to head for the homestead, grab a Diet Coke on the way, and relax... right? Nope. You're not done yet.

I can absolutely, positively tell you that post-workout stretching is the main area I wish I would have paid more attention to when I was younger. Throughout the big years of my career, I had the same routine when I finished my workouts every day. I unloaded the bar, took my shoes off, put on my flip-flops, and went home. I did absolutely no post-workout stretching until I was around 32.

Brothers and sisters, I can't believe how much of a difference it makes. Back in my prime years, I was in a decent amount of pain most of the time. Admittedly, this is just part of being a weightlifter, regardless of your age. If you commit to this sport, you'll live with some pain. It's non-negotiable, and you can't change it. But the exact *level* of pain you live with is definitely something you can change, and I'm going to make you a blood promise that you'll live with less pain if you spend 10-15 minutes stretching after you finish your workouts.

This is when static stretching should be used. When we discussed warming up, I mentioned that static stretching (holding an immobile stretched position for 10-15 seconds) isn't the best way to prepare for a workout. Movement-based ballistic stretching works best at that point. However, after the workout is finished, static stretching is the most beneficial way to increase your muscle recovery and decrease your pain level for the next day. Here are the basic principles you should follow for post-workout stretching:

- Each stretch should be held for 15-20 seconds (I prefer 15).
- You should stretch each muscle group two or three times (15-20 seconds per stretch, repeated 2-3 times).
- The main muscle groups that should be stretched are:
  - Hamstrings
  - Quadriceps
  - Groin
  - Lower back
  - Shoulders
  - Other areas that you particularly have tightness problems with can be stretched as well, but the ones listed above are requirements.

The best stretches for these muscle groups are simple stretches. I'll list some very basic ones, just so you have something to reference in case you know nothing about stretching:

Hamstrings: Straight-leg stretches: Bend down and grab your toes (or as close as you can get), legs straight. Make sure you keep the legs straight and feel the stretch in your hamstrings, not your back.

Quadriceps: Basic quad stretches: Pull your foot up behind you and grab it with your hand, holding on to something stable with your other hand so you don't tip over. Your knee joint should be completely closed, or as close as your flexibility level will allow.

Groin: Lunge position stretches: Position your feet and legs in a long lunge position and push the hip forward, so you feel the stretch in the groin of your rear leg. Alternate legs. Seated butterfly stretches: In a seated position, pull the feet together as close to your body as possible, with the thighs pushed down (by a partner if necessary) towards the floor.

Lower back: Long butterfly stretches: Similar position to the butterfly stretch, except the feet are moved forward (still kept together). The athlete now leans and reaches forward, head towards the feet, and feels the stretch in the lower back.

Shoulders: Shoulder dislocates and pipe rolls with a stick or PVC pipe: These aren't static stretches because they involve movement, but they're still probably the best way to loosen up the shoulders.

As I mentioned when we discussed technique earlier, this book isn't intended to be a comprehensive training manual on all aspects of Olympic weightlifting. *Olympic Weightlifting: A Complete Guide for Athletes and Coaches* by Greg Everett serves that purpose. There's a more detailed section in Greg's book about stretching and flexibility work, and you should use it as a reference if you need additional guidance in this department. For right now, I wanted to accomplish two things:

1. Emphasize the extreme importance of post-workout stretching.
2. Give some basic guidance on how it should be done.

Make this a part of your training. If you don't do this as a masters lifter, you're simply asking for more pain than you need to be dealing with.

SECTION FIVE

Pain Management and Injury Prevention

When you make the decision that this masters weightlifting thing is going to be your path in life, it'll become very clear to you that the actual lifting you do in the gym is only part of your success. The supplemental exercises you use, along with the way you live outside the gym, are going to have an enormous impact on your career. As we've stated before, you could get away with just about anything when you were young. The training you did in the gym was all you really had to think about, because your body was resilient enough to withstand the lack of care you gave it while you were screwing around and eating like crap in your outside life.

Those days are over. You're in a position now where you're simply forced to pay attention to certain things you never had to worry about. If you neglect any of them, you'll pay a price. If you neglect all of them, you might pay the ultimate price. We need to take a careful look at all of these areas. Consider this section a checklist of things you need to be taking good care of, if you expect to have a productive career as a post-25 year old OLifter.

Nutrition

Wow, what a can of worms I just opened. This area has become a massively controversial subject over the years. Sports nutrition is a vast field unto itself, complete with endless amounts of research, study, literature, and conflicting viewpoints about the best way to approach it.

Right from the start, I want to make it clear that I'm not going to unveil any groundbreaking new ideas about how to eat for successful performance. I'm not a nutritionist, nor would I ever claim to have a better opinion than anybody else on this subject. However, I've been an athlete and coach for a very long time at this point, and I'll definitely say that I've learned quite a bit about the right way (and the wrong way) to handle your nutritional life if you're a weightlifter.

Do you want to know the main thing I've observed and learned about sports nutrition over the last 25+ years? It changes a lot, and many people are highly influenced by whatever the current fad is. Because I've been doing this for a long time, I've seen a lot of diets and theories that were supposed to be the next big cutting-edge advancement. Some of them have become enormously popular. Athletes read about a certain nutritional plan, and it sounds awesome because it's supposedly a new spin on things that nobody has thought of before. They try this plan, and they have some success with it. They train well, look good, and feel terrific.

Then the word spreads to thousands of other people. Before you know it, you've got a borderline religious cult. An entire population of people swears that this nutritional method they're using is the BEST and ONLY way to have success as an athlete. People write books about it, more followers get sucked into the fold, and the person who first thought of it makes a butt-load of money.

Years pass by, and the craze rolls merrily forward. But eventually, somebody bursts on the scene with a NEW nutritional theory that sounds different from the old one that everybody was obsessed with. This person has found a new way to reinvent the wheel. It's a departure from the established craze, and it sounds intriguing. By this time, a whole new wave of athletes has found weightlifting and they're all looking for solid advice on how to eat for performance. The old craze is starting to lose momentum because people are always looking for the next big thing, so this new generation of lifters is the prime demographic for a new-fangled nutritional revolution. At this point, the whole cycle simply repeats itself. People try the new diet and experience success, the word spreads, books get written, yadda yadda yadda.

If you stay in this business long enough, you'll see what I'm talking about. However, there's an interesting aspect to this whole scenario that's important to remember. Most of these nutritional crazes promote themselves as the best way to eat for performance. In many cases, the followers get totally carried away and shout from the rooftops that their diet is the ONLY way to eat for performance. They make it sound like they've unlocked the secrets of the universe, and you have to join the revolution if you expect to be successful.

But there's a problem with that mentality, brothers and sisters. You see, people were breaking world records and winning gold medals thirty years ago...and they never even heard of this new dietary method that's supposedly the only path to glory. If the new nutritional craze is a required element of elite performance, how do we explain people who were elite performers back in the 70s and 80s before the craze was even invented? Keep in mind that many of these elite lifters of previous generations were lifting weights that would still be highly competitive at the international level right now. So you can't play the "Well, we've come a long way since the old days" card. The people from the old days, who had no freaking clue about the current nutritional information, lifted weights that would still kick the asses of almost everybody in the world now. So I guess you can't say we've "come a long way." You can only say we've...changed. Those are two different things.

Listen, I'm not arguing against any specific diets or nutritional ideas. If you're using one of them and it works for you, that's terrific. I'm only arguing against the idea that any particular nutritional plan is the chosen one. If you like to eat a certain way, and you're getting results from it, then everything is hunky-dory. Just don't say that YOUR way is the ONLY way...or even the BEST way. It's complex world, and there are many people out there who are also having success (some of them are having a lot more than you) and they do things totally different from you. They've never heard of your diet craze, but they're still successful. That leaves us with only one possible conclusion, and it's the same conclusion we've applied to every other area we've looked at: Many people have good ideas, but nobody has the only idea

Performance vs. Health

As with everything else we've discussed regarding the training of a master lifter, nutrition has to be looked at differently from how younger athletes approach it. This might sound like an odd statement because "eating for performance" sounds like a universal idea, right? Whether you're 21 or 51, you're all human beings, so it should make sense that athletic nutrition applies to everybody the same way. Sounds logical

However, this is another instance when I need to remind you that you're old. Because you're old, you're different. How does this apply to your eating? Older lifters have to be more conscious of their health than younger lifters do, that's how. When athletes are in their twenties, they're a long way from having to worry about things like diabetes, heart disease, cholesterol problems, hypertension, liver disease, etc. Obviously, there are some young people who battle these issues because they've got some kind of genetic predisposition that makes them susceptible. But those are exceptions. For the most part, younger athletes can eat almost anything they want without having to worry about the same complications you start to encounter when you age.

Even with a rudimentary understanding of nutrition and the human body, it should be clear to everybody that diet-related health problems become more concerning as you get older. Young kids can inhale candy, greasy foods, milkshakes, and every other kind of crap under the sun, and most of their levels will still be in a normal range if a doctor draws their blood and measures everything. This changes over time, and most of you are probably already keenly aware of it. As you get older, things like blood sugar, cholesterol levels, blood pressure, etc. can get spiked through the roof when you get irresponsible with your eating. This puts masters athletes in a position where they can't worry ONLY about how nutrition affects their weightlifting results. They have to worry about how nutrition keeps them in a healthy overall condition, away from all the danger zones that lay in wait for us. Let's look at a couple of specific predicaments to illustrate this point:

Another preamble: If you think my discussion of nutrition is going to include a lot of scientific nomenclature and research statistics, you're living in a dream world. I'm going to talk to you like a weightlifter and a coach with an educated background in these fields, not like a scientist.

Carbs and blood sugar: Carbohydrates are a primary energy source for weightlifting. They're most commonly associated with foods and drinks that are high in sugar, and there's a difference between simple carbohydrates and complex carbohydrates. One of the reasons why carbs have developed a bad reputation with some people is their association with sugar. Sugar isn't necessarily a bad thing in all cases, but consuming too much of it obviously raises your blood sugar level. When your blood sugar level goes up and stays up for a long time, you're at a higher level of risk for several health problems including adult-onset diabetes, strokes, etc. Based on this understanding, managing your carb intake (and your blood sugar) is a no-brainer. You need to do it to stay healthy.

Now, here's where this issue gets sticky for weightlifters and athletes. Sugar can be a good source of short-term energy. You've seen those little kids who eat too much sugar and then go completely ballistic, right? Well, that's the kind of situation we're talking about. Weightlifters want to be revved up and full of energy when they train, so many of them will guzzle sugary energy drinks or maybe eat candy bars before they hit the gym, looking for the same physical response as that little kid who's bouncing off the walls.

I've definitely engaged in this practice in the past. Sometimes it works. And as we've already mentioned, there aren't too many risks that go along with it when you're younger. Your body's physiology is very resilient in your early years, and it can return back to normal pretty quickly after you've thrown it out of whack. When you're older, it just doesn't work the same. Sugar rampages can skyrocket your whole system into a dangerous realm. You simply can't use the same "damn the torpedoes" mentality when you're at the age where you could wind up in the hospital if your sugar gets out of control. This is what I'm talking about when I say older lifters have to be conscious of much more than just performance benefits of nutrition. They can't just think about lifting big weights. They also have to think about not dying.

Bodyweight: Let me give you a personal story to illustrate this one. I mentioned to you earlier that I've had a couple of knee surgeries over the last few years, remember? Okay, so here's what happened. On the day I went in for my first knee surgery in 2011, the nurses took me in the back and put me on the operating table, and then they drew some of my blood. They wanted to check all my levels to make sure I was healthy before they knocked me out and started the surgery—pretty standard stuff. After lying in the bed and waiting forever (normal procedure with surgeries), the nurse came to me and said, "Your blood sugar is extremely high. We can do the operation, but you need to see your doctor after you've recovered. Your sugar is almost diabetic-level."

Needless to say, this scared the crap out of me. I got the operation done and then went in to see my surgeon a week later for my first post-op checkup. My surgeon works in the same practice with my regular doctor, so I was able to talk to him as well. He reiterated what the nurse had told me. My blood sugar was in a dangerous range. If it were much higher, I would be diagnosed as a diabetic. I asked the doc what I needed to do to straighten this out, and he gave me the normal input about a better diet and exercise. He also told me that losing some bodyweight would help a lot. I was 39 years old at the time.

Because this had me worried, I made some big changes right away. My bodyweight at this time was hovering between 275-280 lbs, which was the heaviest I've even been in my life. I was very strong at this bodyweight, but admittedly I was carrying a lot of fat in my gut. Over the next few months after the surgery, I went through the physical therapy to get my knee healthy again, but I also made some big changes in my diet to drop some weight. I naturally lose weight easily, so it wasn't hard to do. After a few months, I was back down to a comfortable 260 lbs and I went back in to get my blood checked again. Fortunately, my numbers were back to normal and I was in the clear. I've continued to maintain the same bodyweight, right around the 259-260 range, ever since then and my checkups have all been okay.

For many weightlifters, bodyweight is a big issue. Many of us try to stay as big as possible when we're training because the extra mass benefits our lifting. But once again, this is an example of an area where performance benefits have to be balanced with health status. I was stronger at 280 than I am at 260, no doubt about it. My strength (and my competition totals) has taken a hit from reducing my bodyweight, but I'm healthier now than I used to be. Since I want to live a long life, health is a priority. I can't just think about how much weight I can lift. There's more to it, at this point.

Examples of Trends

Now that we understand the proper perspective on how you should approach nutrition as a masters athlete, we're left with the question, "Which diet should I be following to become a good weightlifter and stay healthy? HOW should I eat to accomplish both of these things?"

We've already mentioned dietary trends. Athletes, like everybody else, are always susceptible to the latest craze... the new revolutionary approach to eating that will transform you into a golden god. In fact, let's take a look at a few of the ones I've heard of since I've been in weightlifting:

The Fit for Life Diet: This one was all the rage in the 1980s. A couple of alleged health gurus wrote a book called *Fit for Life*, and it was a bestseller. There was a dietary approach in there, based on principles like:

- Carbs and proteins shouldn't be eaten in the same meal
- Dairy is a major no-no
- Water shouldn't be drunk at mealtimes

As I said, this was a bestseller...

The Zone Diet: This one popped up in the 1990s. A biochemist named Barry Sears built an empire, wrote books, and made a fortune from his nutritional approach. The Zone Diet is aimed at keeping your body's hormonal levels in an appropriate "zone" by eating a ratio of 40% carbs, 30% protein, and 30% fat. Its popularity grew to the point where people simply started calling it "the 40-30-30 plan."

The Atkins Diet: The Atkins frenzy skyrocketed around 2003. It's a low-carb plan, obviously much different from the Zone. Ten years ago, you couldn't take a deep breath without hearing somebody talk about the damn Atkins Diet. It basically made carbohydrates look like tools of Satan.

The Paleo Diet Aaahhh, now we're talking. As I write this book in 2014, our society is currently in the clutches of the Paleo Diet. If the term "paleo" sounds familiar, that's because you heard it in high school when you were learning about dinosaurs. The basic idea with this diet is that we should only eat foods that were on the earth thousands of years ago during the caveman era. I'm simplifying it greatly and I'm sure some Paleo druids will froth at the mouth if I leave out any important details, but we're basically working with the understanding that modern processed foods are bad for you. We should eat what our Stone Age ancestors ate if we want to be healthy. In other words, fish and vegetables are okay because cavemen were eating them. Cavemen weren't eating cream cheese, so you can't have that.

You've probably heard of these diets, right? Most of you are 30 or older, which means these might ring a bell. People who are 21 years old in 2014 have probably only heard of the Paleo diet because it's the current craze, but they start to pile up if you stay in the game for a long time. Now let me give you another diet that used to be pretty popular:

The Graham Diet: This nutritional plan was invented by a man named Sylvester Graham, who was born in 1794 and died in 1851. The Graham Diet was a vegetarian plan that focused almost entirely on fruits, vegetables, whole wheat foods and water (no meats, almost no dairy). Graham believed that this diet would stop people from having inappropriate sexual thoughts and masturbating. He considered masturbation to be a cause for blindness, so his dietary plan was developed to stop everybody from pleasuring themselves. (I'm not kidding about this, by the way. He's also the guy who invented the graham cracker.)

In case you don't get the point, let me just state it very clearly. Special diets are nothing new. They've been around for hundreds of years and there will be many more as time rolls on. The people who invent them can convince you that their diet will prevent everything from diabetes to heart attacks to jerking off. The question is, "Do any of these diets work? Are they effective?"

Once again, the answer is entirely individual. If you follow a special diet and it works for you... then it works. Nobody has a monopoly on this stuff. Some people feel great and lift well when they're following the Zone Diet. Others get the same positive results from the Paleo Diet. Many people (like me) don't follow any special regimen. We simply use basic nutritional principles to eat a balanced diet, without aligning it with any particular name or method. I guess the conclusion to all this is the idea that you need to eat healthy if you want to live well and have athletic success. There are many different ways to do it, plain and simple. If you stick to a lot of fundamental rules about sports nutrition, you'll probably get exactly what you need. Here are some the main ones you should know about:

Protein: Protein intake is a no-brainer for everybody. Your body needs it for recovery, growth, and overall health. The best places to get your daily protein are whole foods, like lean meats and eggs. People talk a lot about protein powder and those protein bars with jazzy names like Big Colossal Mega Protein Hunk 500. These products can be useful supplements to your diet, but they shouldn't be used in place of foods. Athletes have been using protein shakes to gain bodyweight for years. Protein shakes come in all forms, usually combining protein powder with milk, eggs, and a variety of other things like bananas, maybe some ice cream, etc. The goal with these things is to pack on bodyweight, and they're mostly used by younger athletes who have fast metabolism. They want to build as much muscle mass as possible, so they have to ram extra protein and calories down their throats because their youthful metabolism is burning like a flamethrower. I don't know many masters athletes who drink high-calorie protein shakes because our metabolism is so much slower when we're older. Many masters have to work in the opposite direction, refining their diets to keep away from the flabby body fat gains that can happen easily as you get older and your metabolism starts to creep along like a garden slug.

Fruits and vegetables: Very few people argue against the necessity and positive results of consuming fruits and vegetables. They're probably one of the most agreed-upon areas in the field. They provide outstanding combinations of unrefined carbohydrates, vitamins and minerals that are essential for recovery without the potential problems that go along with processed foods. Many nutritionists say "the darker the better" when referring to the color of vegetables. This is yet another area I neglected when I was younger. Back in my top lifting years, the only vegetables I ate were the ones Burger King put on my cheeseburger. Now, as an old person, I eat tons of them and I feel a lot better all the time. Funny how that works.

Balance: As we've already alluded to, athletes need to make sure they're getting protein, carbohydrates, and fats in their diets. Despite any propaganda you might have heard, you don't want to eliminate any of these basic nutritional elements. Now, it's important to keep a clear overall perspective of your diet. In other words, where is your protein coming from? Where are your carbs coming from? Where is your fat coming from? These are individualized questions, and you have to take a look at how you eat on a regular basis to answer them. If you're so consumed with the idea of everything being fat-free and sugar-free, you might be throwing your body out of whack. You have to get fats from somewhere, people. They're important. The same thing goes for carbs. Sometimes, I think people simply get obsessed with protein, protein, and more protein. This can lead to neglect in other areas. All you really have to do is read some basic information about nutritional guidelines and then structure your eating so you're covering all the bases. Don't try to erase something from your diet if it's widely considered to be a necessary human element.

Hydration: You want to know something I've noticed over the years? Many people get insanely consumed with their nutritional plans, and they simultaneously neglect their water intake. It blows my mind when I hear this. Personally, I've found hydration to be just as important (or more) than nutrition. When my diet gets junky and undisciplined for a few days because I'm busy with work or something, I don't really notice a drastic physical change. But if I neglect my water intake, I feel it pretty quickly. If you're an athlete, you simply have to drink a lot of water and many athletes don't drink enough…plain and simple.

Sports supplements: Yikes! This topic is enormous and it can go on forever. If you've had any experience as an athlete, you've discovered that sports supplements are a bazillion-dollar industry. Powders, pills, gels, drinks, more pills…the list never ends. If you walk into someplace like GNC (General Nutrition Center), it becomes a sensory-overload situation. Your brain gets assaulted with every kind of supplement you could ever imagine, and every single one of them claims to make you a superior athlete. In addition, some of the descriptions of these supplements are downright bizarre. You'll read a brochure about a new protein powder or pill, and it tells you how this particular product is highly advanced because it's made from a crystallized blend of sarsaparilla root and panther testicles. If you take it, it'll increase your muscle mass by 64% in three weeks. All you have to do is cough up the $59.99 for a 90-day supply and, before you know it, you'll look like the bodybuilding freak on the label (the guy with the crew-cut and enormous biceps, screaming at you while he does dumbbell curls). Listen folks, I've been lifting weights for most of my life and I've tried several of these things. You want my personal opinion? Most of them are a waste of money. I honestly think you can get everything you need from the proper diet. As we've mentioned several times, it's all individual. If you take the panther-testicle pills and they seem to make you stronger, that's wonderful. But I've blown a lot of money (mostly in my younger years, when I was a gullible kid) on these things, and I can't say I ever found anything that really made a big difference.

Nutritional supplements: These are a little different from the crazy sports supplements. These are products like fish oil, multi-vitamins, herbal medicine, etc. They're not marketed as get-stronger bodybuilding supplements. They're more directed towards overall health and biological improvements, for lack of a better term.

> **Fish oil:** You've probably heard about this stuff, right? This is a nutritional supplement that usually comes in softgel pills, and it contains oil from the tissues of fish. Fish oil provides your body with omega-3 fatty acids. A lot of research has been done on this product, and the potential health benefits are tremendous. Fish oil has been shown to reduce inflammation in the body, which is one of the main reasons athletes like it so much—it helps fight the

swelling that comes from hard workouts. It has also been shown to have possible benefits in preventing heart disease, hypertension, and several other health problems. I started taking fish oil when I was 36 or 37, and I wish I would have been taking it my whole life. It's one of the few things I've taken that actually make a noticeable difference and I recommend to everybody, athlete or not.

Glucosamine: This is a dietary supplement that's mainly marketed towards adults as a product that strengthens your joints. It's often combined with something called chondroitin, with the idea that the two work well together. If you go to a pharmacy store, you'll see rows and rows of pill bottles with the words glucosamine and chondroitin on the labels. The basic theory with this stuff is that it strengthens cartilage and connective tissue in the body's joints. Studies have been done on its effectiveness and there are some conflicted results, but it's extremely popular. I personally use it, and I strongly believe that it works.

Multi-vitamins: Everybody knows about these. They're pills that combine a wide range of dietary essentials (vitamins A, B, C, etc.) and they supposedly make sure your body is getting the proper daily amount of each. They're extremely popular, although the research on their effectiveness has been mixed. Many people will take specific vitamin supplements if they're naturally deficient in a particular area. Some people don't take them at all.

Caffeine: Ouch, it's getting personal now. Some of you get downright defensive when I mention the word "caffeine." You act like I'm talking about one of your children, for God's sake. That's because some of you are as attached to your caffeine as you are to your own kids, if we really want to be truthful about it. Caffeine is a stimulant that's commonly found in coffee, soft drinks, energy drinks, etc. Our society is pathetically dependent on it. Starbucks coffee houses are treated like first-aid stations. Many people can't function properly if they don't have their morning coffee. It's ridiculous, isn't it? It's a slightly modified version of coke addicts who can't get revved up enough to make it through the day unless they snort a few lines. Seriously...just change the laws and the severity associated with these two products, and they're practically the same.

As with all drugs, caffeine is something you build a tolerance to. If you ingest it long enough, the effects start to wear thin and you need a more powerful shot to get the desired energy spike. You can also go overboard with it, slurping down too much and winding up a twitchy wreck with a blood pressure reading that could get you admitted to the emergency room. Energy drinks like Red Bull, Monster, and others have given us the opportunity go high-octane on the caffeine rampage. Screw your morning coffee. Man up and slam some Red Bulls. It's like graduating from weed to meth. The short-term energy benefits to athletes are obvious, which is why all of this stuff is so incredibly popular. And even though I'm writing about it from an ivory tower, I'm guilty too. I like Monster energy drinks. I don't guzzle them continually throughout the day, but I like them and I'll use them in moderation to get my motor running. The risk of dependency on caffeine is extremely high, which is exactly what Starbucks wants. They're looking for lifetime customers, so step right up and join the revolution baby...

Performance-Enhancing Drugs

Wow, this is a drastically abrupt U-turn from our analysis of sports nutrition, huh? We've been sitting around, having this nice mellow chat about eating our little vegetables and chicken breasts and then BAM!! Now we're talking about DRUGS!! It's like getting sucker punched. Actually, I think the discussion of caffeine is a good transition into this murky area. This is a book about Olympic weightlifting, and it would be silly to cower away from the subject of steroids and performance-enhancing drugs. It's the 500 lb elephant in the room, and I see no reason to avoid it. However, I'm going to keep the conversation limited.

We're going to use the abbreviation PED (performance-enhancing drugs) to make this easier to read. PEDs, in weightlifting and sports terminology, are a very broad range of pharmaceutical drugs and other substances that are engineered to improve an athlete's performance through higher testosterone production, nervous system stimulation, pain killing, and other physical avenues. When laypeople hear about these substances, they automatically think about anabolic steroids because it's the most common association. Steroids, using the simplest possible explanation, are used to make athletes stronger. Other drugs like amphetamines or "speed" can be used to get athletes cranked up for training or competition. Diuretics can be used to drain water out of the body, usually by athletes who need to lose weight in order to make a specific bodyweight class. There's also a thing called "blood doping," which is a way of boosting the amount of red blood cells and oxygen in the athlete's bloodstream, increasing endurance. Long-distance athletes like cyclists are notorious for doing this stuff, often through a drug called EPO. There are various other physiological methods for using PEDs to elevate performance, but these are the primary ones.

Most of the PEDs that provide any substantial advantage are illegal in sports. This is done because sports organizations believe the use of PEDs is unfair and dangerous to the athletes' health. All Olympic sports conduct drug testing to make sure the athletes are clean. Most other major sports, like professional football and baseball, also use drug testing with their athletes. If athletes take PEDs and fail the drug tests, they're usually suspended for substantial lengths of time as a punishment for breaking the rules.

PED use has become a global obsession in sports. The use of drugs by athletes to gain a competitive advantage is very common, and has been for decades. Sports that involve strength and power are most closely connected with PEDs because of the incredible muscle-building capabilities that come from steroid use. Weightlifting, as you probably already know, is one of the biggest culprits in the PED lexicon. Many weightlifters use PEDs, and they get to experience huge competitive gains as their muscles get stronger and their training recovery time gets minimized. Various forms of testosterone are the drug of choice for many weightlifters.

If an athlete takes PEDs in a controlled manner with some kind of medical supervision, it's very possible to pass drug tests while taking them. In other words, there are ways to break the rules and not get caught. This is common practice in most of the top weightlifting countries in the world. Athletes who stay clean and refuse to take PEDs are at a massive competitive disadvantage when they face athletes who are "on the juice." If you're not familiar with informal sports jargon, "juicing" is the most common terminology for PED use.

Believe it or not, PED use isn't confined only to young athletes who are in the prime of their Olympic or professional careers. That's right my friends, masters athletes use them too. Drug testing is done at the masters level, but not as stringently as it's done with younger Olympic-level athletes. Drug testing costs a lot of money, and the International Olympic Committee has made the totally understandable decision that the money for testing needs to be spent more at the Olympic level than the masters division. In other words, they're a lot more worried about young elite athletes than a bunch of grey-skinned old geezers who still want to hit the juice.

This creates a situation where it's easy to get away with PED use when you're a master, plain and simple. So, how many masters weightlifters are juicing? Nobody knows the answer to that. I think PED use is fairly common in the masters division. It's not as rampant as it is in the professional level of Olympic competition, but it's still there. I personally know many masters lifters who take PEDs. Some of them are honest about it, and others lie their asses off.

I'm not planning to give you any soapbox preaching about PEDs. However, I'll offer a few thoughts that you can take any way you like. I've definitely chosen a side of this issue, but I also completely understand that the world is complex and there are a lot of grey areas out there.

Cheating: Are athletes cheating when they take PEDs? Well, PEDs are illegal in drug-tested sports. That means it's against the rules to take them. When somebody breaks the rules of a sport to gain a competitive advantage over somebody else, that's basically the dictionary definition of cheating. Any analysis of "cheating" that goes beyond the basic definition is all going to be influenced by the personal opinions and ideas of the individual who is looking at it. Additionally, there's also the question of whether athletes even care about the cheating issue. Some do, and some don't.

Health risks: Most pharmaceutical substances involve some kind of potential adverse side effects. However, these side effects are usually connected with excessive use or "abuse" of the drug. Many PEDs, like any other drug, can be taken responsibly and relatively safely if their use is carefully monitored by a qualified expert. However, many athletes take PEDs on their own, without any guidance or control. This becomes abuse of the drug, which is where health risks begin to surface. I know lifters who have been taking PEDs for decades without any major health problems. And I also know lifters who have suffered serious side effects from them. As with everything else, it's an individual thing.

For the record, I am against the use of PEDs. Throughout my top competitive years, I was a 100% clean athlete who never took any kind of banned substances. Like all clean athletes, this held my career back because many of my competitors were juicing. It angered me, but I didn't let it drive me out of the sport and I try not to hold any grudges against people who didn't follow the same rules. I'll conclude this section with a few short statements that sum up the issue for me, personally.

- Regardless of any individual philosophies or arguments, breaking the rules to gain a competitive advantage is generally going to be considered wrong by most people. You can make up your own mind about what that statement means to you. Your interpretation of it is your business.
- Taking any kind of drug without sensible planning and responsibility can lead to damaging health consequences. I strongly encourage everybody to take care of their bodies and minds in the best way possible.

End of discussion.

Therapeutic Exercises and Prehab

We've talked about nutrition, supplements, and pharmaceuticals (both legal and banned), so now we want to shift towards the kind of exercises you should be doing to keep your body healthy. The things we just looked at were nutritional supplements. Think of this next section as workout supplements. We've mentioned several times that your joints and your flexibility start to get a little stiffer when you age, and that means your workout regimen has to include additional measures to address this problem.

Specifically, what am I talking about? I'm talking about the boring crap you don't like to do. Assistance exercises with bands, stability balls, light dumbbells, etc. That's what this section is about, and I just heard a collective GROAN from many of you. You don't like doing this stuff because you'd rather go to the gym and do heavy OLifts and squats. You're in this game because you like lifting heavy barbells, and that's ALL you want to do. If you're stubborn, you probably neglect pain-management assistance exercises entirely. You lift heavy weights and then you walk out of the gym and go home. Great, excellent, you're a tyrannosaurus... impervious to the laws of nature. If you're still relatively young, you might be getting away with this behavior. If you can get away with it forever, then praise the lord and pass the ammunition. You might be one of those genetic freaks we talked about. However, you need to remember that a couple of things are probably (most likely) going to happen to you if you keep blowing off pain-management assistance:

1. You'll be in constant pain, and it'll limit your career.
2. You'll eventually get driven out of the sport completely, possibly because of injury.

If those things don't sound peachy to you, then you need to pull your head out of your rectum and start thinking about adding some kind of therapy work to your training regimen. Let's look at some of the best ways to do it.

Body Parts & Your Personal Issues

Human beings are physically diverse, and that means different people will hurt in different areas. Here's a quick list of the body parts that endure the most stress in Olympic lifting:

1. Knees
2. Lower back
3. Shoulders
4. Elbows
5. Wrists

You're chuckling right now, asking, "Hell, is there anything left?" Sure there is. The OLifts are total-body exercises, and everything from the soles of your feet to your fingernails are susceptible to pain and soreness. But the primary culprit areas are the ones I just listed. You have to ask yourself which areas are the most problematic for you, personally. Some people have knees that are perfectly flexible and stable, and they rarely have any pain or soreness in them. Others have excellent elbow mechanisms that provide the perfect blend of mobility and solid lockout. In other words, some people don't have to worry much about particular areas.

However, almost everybody who sticks with OLifting for the long haul starts to develop some nagging pain and soreness in one (or several) of these problem areas. Maybe we're talking about a lifter who never notices a twinge of pain in the lower back, but his wrists are constantly inflamed and aching. Or maybe we're talking about another dude (or dudette) who is in perfect working order from the waist up, but the knees are a major obstacle. Your job as an athlete is to take regular inventories of your body and determine if you've got any specific problems that need some kind of attention. When these things pop up, there are a couple of different categories they fall into:

- Pain issues that don't require special exercises: These are the types of problems that can be solved simply through stretching, icing, or some other kind of passive method.
- Pain issues that require special exercises: These are the problems that won't go away unless you add some kind of active exercise to strengthen (or loosen up) the area.

Prehab: This is a term you need to be familiar with. Everybody has heard the word "rehab" in some context. If you're an alcoholic or drug addict, "rehab" might refer to a program that gets you sober. If you're talking about physical issues, "rehab" refers to the rehabilitative work you have to do in order to make your body healthy again after some kind of injury or surgery. In other words, rehab is what takes place AFTER a problem has occurred. "Prehab" is the practice of doing some kind of work to PREVENT a problem from happening in the first place. If you incorporate prehab exercises into your workout regimen, it means you're doing special exercises that are designed to keep you from getting hurt, as opposed to using rehab exercises after the hurt has happened.

Equipment: Now, we need to look at some tools and equipment that are commonly used in the areas of pain management and prehab:

> **Ice**: Simplest thing in the world. Using ice to reduce swelling and control pain is the oldest trick in the book, and also one of the most reliable. There are a variety of ways to apply ice to a swollen, painful area. The easiest way is to fill a thin plastic bag with ice and just stick it where you're hurting for 20 minutes (I've heard different recommendations for the length of time you should ice, but I've been using 20-minute intervals throughout my whole career). Make sure the bag is THIN. I've seen a few people who wrap a towel around a bag of ice before they put it on their ankle or knee. What a waste of time. You basically wind up sitting there with a mild cooling sensation, which is doing nothing to reduce swelling or pain. That ice should be...ice cold. It's not comfortable, but you can't be a wimp with this stuff. Some people also like ice massage, which is where you fill little Styrofoam cups with water and freeze them, and then massage the painful area with the frozen chunk of ice, tearing away the Styrofoam as the ice progressively melts. Ice baths are another

option, and they're as simple as they sound. Fill a big tub with cold water and ice, and then jump in. Personally, I ice all the time, even when I'm not battling an injury. I use it as prehab, just 20 minutes of ice on my knees at night while I'm watching TV. It's not terribly inconvenient and believe me, there's a hell of a payoff when I come to the gym and my knees don't hurt.

Stretching: I'm adding this to the list because it belongs here, but I won't go into any real description of stretching because we've covered it earlier in the book.

Exercise balls: Some people call these stability balls. These are plastic inflated balls that can be used to perform a wide range of exercises. Sitting on them or doing exercises on them, like sit-ups for example, requires several muscles to stay engaged because of the soft, loose nature of the ball. Instead of doing abdominal crunches on the floor, where your abdominal muscles are the only ones contracting, doing the crunches on an exercise ball will force your abs, lower back, hips, and other muscles to stay activated simply to avoid tipping over and falling off the ball. Stability balls also come in disc shapes, so you can stand on them and work the muscles of your feet, ankles, and lower legs.

Resistance bands: These look like big rubber bands. They have varying degrees of thickness, along with several options such as handles. Bands are very common in physical therapy because they can be used for an extremely wide range of exercises that can improve range of motion while also strengthening the muscles around a joint, such as the shoulder.

Massage balls: These are balls of all shapes and sizes, and you can use them to massage yourself. Most of them are roughly the size of a tennis ball. If you've ever had massage therapy, you remember the uncomfortable sensation when the therapist was digging his/her elbows into your muscles to loosen them up. Massage balls mimic that action, but you can use them when you're alone, simply by lying down on them. If you've got a sore lower back, for example, you can place the massage ball on the floor and then simply lay down on it, moving your body around so the ball massages the afflicted area.

Theracanes: Some people call these "back knobbers." These things look like big iron hooks with a round knob on the end. The idea is that you can grab them and stick the end of the hook behind you, then put it where you've got tightness and pain and use your hands to work the hook around and basically self-massage the area. Once again, it's intended to imitate the action of massage therapists digging their elbows into your knotty areas.

Foam rollers: This is a big solid tube of compressed foam that's used for something called self-myofascial release (a fancy term for getting your muscles to loosen up). You lie down on a foam roller and...roll around on it. The force of your bodyweight pushes the sore area down onto the roller as you move back and forth on it, allowing the roller to aggressively massage and relax the tight tissue. This is a great way of getting stiff muscles to loosen up, and it's very common among athletes of all sports.

Therapy sticks: These look like rolling pins...the kind your mom used to flatten dough. You grab the handles on the end, just like a rolling pin, and roll the stick across a stiff area of your body to loosen up the muscles. It's basically the same kind of movement as a foam roller.

There are other kinds of equipment in this area. It's all very easy to find online and almost all of it is accompanied by some kind of instructions that show you how to use it properly. The ones I've listed above are probably the most common ones I see among weightlifters.

Programming Prehab Exercises into Your Workouts

I'm going to take a revolutionary approach to this next section. Now that I've described the importance of therapeutic exercise and listed some possible equipment you can use to get it done, you're all asking the same thing. "Okay, what kind of exercises should we use, and how do we do them?"

Instead of including a section with a long list of exercises and photos that show you how to do them, I'm simply going to give you a list of websites you can visit to get the information you need. How's that for staying current with the times? Seriously, professional organizations that specialize in physical therapy and prehab exercises can do a much better job than I can when it comes to teaching you the stuff you need to know. Here are some useful places that give you the instruction and guidance you need to incorporate therapeutic exercises and prehab into your training:

HEP2GO.com (www.hep2go.com) This is an enormously comprehensive website for physical therapists, athletic trainers, etc. with tons of information and photos that show you how to use the exact kind of exercises we're talking about. They break down their site according to body parts, offering instruction that's easy to read and great visual examples. You can find a therapeutic exercise for just about anything on there.

Orthopedic Specialists of North Carolina (www.orthonc.com/physical-therapy/home-exercise-protocols) Like HEP2GO, this is a website with a very wide range of exercises and plans for helping with your painful problems. This site actually offers a few additional ideas for older people who might be having physical problems that aren't necessarily sports-related. Some of you geezers might be able to find some good stuff on here.

Band-Exercises.net (www.band-exercises.net) This is a big comprehensive site with all things related to resistance band training. Very easy to navigate and useful.

Tennis Ball Massage (http://saveyourself.ca/articles/tennis-ball.php) How to use a simple tennis ball (and other types) to work out your back pain.

Needless to say, there are hundreds of other sites where you can get terrific input on how to use prehab and therapy exercises to improve your body's health. I understand that websites come and go, so there's a possibility that the ones I just gave you might vanish at some point. I hope this book lasts for generations. It would be awesome if masters weightlifters in the year 2094 are still reading it. If that happens, the sites I just gave you might be shut down. But here's the thing…it took me about 5 minutes to find these sites. I simply typed things like "physical therapy exercises" or "massage ball techniques" into Google, and I was led straight to them. To make a long story short, I'm basically referring you to the experts. I know how important this stuff is and I know how to use it, but it's not my primary area of study. You should seek out the best perspectives if you decide to utilize these resources, and they're very easy to find.

In addition, I need to mention the idea of actually finding a professional to work with if you've got a significant problem. It's fine to do your own research and you can get some good help that way, but it's much more beneficial to find a physical therapist and let them teach you what you need to do. PTs are all over the place, and most of the ones I've worked with have been excellent. If it's possible, you should try to find professionals who have some understanding of what weightlifting is. Believe me, it can be pretty damn frustrating to work with a doctor who has no bloody clue what OLifting is or how to deal with it. Years ago, I was having some knee trouble that wouldn't go away, so I went to a doctor to get checked out. I described my weightlifting training in detail and asked for some input on how I could manage my knee pain. His response was, "Well, can you just use machines from now on?" I felt like kicking the guy in the nuts.

When I was going through the physical therapy for my ACL surgeries, I learned a lot of exercises to strengthen not only my knee joints, but the areas AROUND my knees. That's a pretty important point in this discussion. If you're having pain in a certain area, it might not necessarily be coming from a problem with that area. It might be coming from a problem with another muscle/connective tissue group that's connected to the area. For example, let's say your knees hurt and you can't figure out what the cause is. Obviously, there's a chance that you might have a structural issue within the actual knee joint. However, there's also a possibility that the pain might be caused by something else, such as your IT bands. In case you don't know, your IT (iliotibial) bands are long strips of connective tissue that run down the outsides of your thighs, from your hip to your knee. If these bands are tight and irritated, they can actually pull the muscles of your lower quadriceps (and possibly your knee cap) out of position, causing knee pain. Now we have a situation where your knees hurt, but it's not because there's anything wrong with them. The problem is in a surrounding area, and it's easy to fix. You have to loosen up those IT bands.

I've continued to use several of the exercises I learned when I was getting PT after my surgeries. They're permanent parts of my workout routine now. They take up some time and they aren't terribly exciting, but they're effective. I want to continue doing this sport for a long time, and I'm willing to do some boring PT work if it extends my career. It might behoove you to think the same way, if you're interested in longevity. If you don't give a crap about any of that and you're just gonna go balls to the wall until the plane crashes into the mountain, don't worry about any of this. Just slam a bunch of Red Bulls and flail away. I'm sure it'll work, for a little while. Eventually you'll be reduced to a quivering puddle of oily discharge, but that was your life plan all along...right?

Massage Therapy and Chiropractic

This section doesn't need to be very long because it's basically just a recommendation to take advantage of these areas, especially massage. Most of the top-level weightlifting programs in the world use massage therapy as a mandatory component of how they train their athletes. I was just reading an interview the other day with Russian lifter Tatiana Kashirina, who is currently the World Champion in the 75+ kg category and the strongest female OLifter on the planet. She gets three massages every week, no exceptions. I've heard the same statements from many Olympic competitors.

It's amazing how helpful massage therapy is. Obviously, it has to be the right kind of massage. There are several different techniques, ranging from Swedish massage (slow, gentle stroking) to deep-tissue massage (hard, penetrating massage with thumbs and elbows). Generally, most weightlifters get the highest benefit from deep-tissue work. Our training is hard and heavy, so our massages need to be hard and heavy too, generally speaking.

Massage therapy costs money, unless you've got some kind of special deal worked out with somebody. It also requires time (most good sessions last 60 minutes). Time and money...those two things aren't a good combination for busy adults with careers and families. I understand how inconvenient it can be to work this stuff into your schedule. However, three massages a week probably isn't what we're talking about for you. If you can get three per week, that's paradise. But most of us will be struggling to find the time and money for two massages per month. Hey, anything is better than nothing. Getting two massages per month will be extremely helpful in your training. And no matter how busy you are, you can scrounge up two hours every thirty days if you really make it a priority.

Chiropractic care is a different field. In layman's terms, massage therapy is where you get rubbed and prodded, while chiropractic treatment is where you get popped and cracked. Chiropractors use manual techniques to adjust the joints and soft tissue of your body, primarily the spine. The basic idea is that your body gets tight and twisted through hard training (and life in general) and eventually you're walking around in pain because your muscles and joints are all out of alignment. Chiropractors work to relax and align your joints again so the pain decreases. That's an extremely rudimentary analysis, but you get the basic idea. Many people swear by chiropractic treatment. They get huge benefits from it and their quality of life improves. There are millions of chiropractors in the world, so obviously it's legitimate.

In terms of weightlifting, I've heard mixed reviews over the years. Personally, it's not a field I've looked into very deeply. I had a little chiropractic treatment years ago, and I wasn't impressed with the results. But I know some lifters who like it a lot. I've known more lifters who migrate towards massage therapy over chiropractic, generally. Please don't think I'm disrespecting the chiropractic field, by the way. Some of you who are reading this might be chiropractors, and you're having a hissy fit now because you think I'm minimizing the importance of what you do. Not true. I've heard from weightlifters over the years who love it, so I totally respect the value of it.

There are several other kinds of treatment methods out there, like acupuncture and active release techniques (ART). It's certainly not a bad idea to explore any of these. Who knows, one of them might be the magic formula for you. As with our entire discussion throughout this book, it's all individual.

NSAIDs and Painkillers

I want to cover just a couple more areas in this section, and once again I'm going to use some previously published material to address them. The first area is painkillers, which is a topic that's important to examine. The following passage is an excerpt from a Performance Menu article I wrote for Catalyst Athletics on the subject. Some of you have read it, many of you haven't. So here it is, and it basically sums up my opinion about the subject.

You Have No Idea How This Feels

Excerpt from Performance Menu issue #77, June 1 2011

Painkillers. Let's just go ahead and talk about them. Most of you probably know what NSAIDs are (nonsteroidal anti-inflammatory drugs). These are legal drugs that reduce inflammation and pain. Ibuprofen is probably the most common NSAID for athletes and the general population because it works and it can be bought anywhere. Stronger NSAIDs, such as Diclofenac and Nabumetone, usually have to be obtained from a hospital with a prescription. These bad boys work pretty well, but there are some health risks if they are used excessively. Gastrointestinal problems are fairly common, and some research has determined that there can be potential problems with the liver and kidneys. However, the dosages would usually have to be pretty high and long-term for these problems to arise. There are also the "high octane" painkillers, such as morphine and other opioids. You're on your own if you want to start rolling the dice with these. There are going to be drug-testing problems with them if you compete, and the list of adverse effects is pretty long and scary.

Here's my personal experience and basic philosophy on painkillers. When I was in the biggest years of my competitive career, I relied pretty heavily on NSAIDs such as Voltaren and Cataflam (these are trade names of Diclofenac). These are all legal substances in weightlifting, so I wasn't breaking any rules by taking them. The weightlifting team I trained with had one of the toughest programs in the United States, and the workload was just plain brutal. At the risk of sounding arrogant, I doubt if there were many people in this country who were training as hard as we were. Looking back now, I don't know if I could have kept up with the training demands without the NSAIDs. I didn't care much about health risks because my mentality was, "You do whatever you have to do (legally) to get bigger lifts." Now, I'm thirty-eight years old and my training workload is greatly reduced from what it used to be. With the type of programming I use now, I hit the ibuprofen for two or three weeks when I'm in the toughest phase of a training cycle (usually the weeks leading up to a meet). That's about it. By the way, I've never had any health problems from the NSAID use.

I would never recommend that anyone develop a dependence on any type of drug, including NSAIDs. The potential health risks from long-term use have been documented. But I also can't preach to anyone about complete abstinence from painkillers because I believe that the life of a serious weightlifter can sometimes demand it. The athlete and the coach have to have a very clear set of goals, and they also have to have a very clear definition of what they're willing to do to achieve those goals. Do painkillers work? Yes. Are there health risks associated with them? Yes. Can they get you through the most difficult times of your training life? Yes. Can they have negative effects? Yes. That's all I have to say about it, brothers and sisters. You're all adults and you can make your own decisions.

Supportive Equipment

In Olympic weightlifting, there are only a few kinds of supportive equipment you can use. They include:

- Weightlifting shoes
- Belts
- Wrist wraps (or tape)
- Tape on the fingers or hands
- Knee sleeves or wraps
- Lifting straps (Straps aren't actually supportive equipment that you can use in competition. They're a form of training equipment, but I'll include them just for the sake of covering all the bases.)

Once again, I'm going to use a piece of previously published information because it sums up my opinion about the issue pretty well.

Wraps, Belts, and Straps

Excerpt from Catalyst Athletics website, October 15, 2012

BELTS: My personal preference is to use a belt only for clean and jerks, squats, and deadlifts (rack jerks and clean pulls are included in that too). And I only put the belt on when I go above 80ish% in these exercises. For example, my best back squat when I was doing my top lifting was usually around 240-250 kilos. My rule back in those days was that I only used a belt when

I went over 200. When I was clean and jerking 180, I only put the belt on when I went 150 or above, etc. I think many lifters use these same general guidelines, because lifting without a belt is one of the most effective ways to strengthen the core muscles in your torso. Most lifters don't like to use a belt in the snatch (including me), but there are some that do. There's certainly nothing wrong with it as long as the bar doesn't hit the buckle on the way up. Some lifters don't use one at all, for anything. The heaviest clean and jerk of all time was done without a belt and the vast majority of lifters don't use it for the snatch. It's just a matter of personal preference. I also think Olympic lifters should use Olympic lifting belts. Thick powerlifting belts can screw up your bottom position because they're bulky. They also make you look like you don't know which sport you're in when you go to meets. Also, I only use belts with a buckle. Maybe I'm too old-school, but I just can't find a way to trust velcro belts.

WRIST WRAPS: I've used wrist wraps on and off throughout my career. When I was doing my biggest lifting, I didn't use them. I'm using them now because I'm getting old and things hurt more than they used to. Basically, I think you should use them as a last resort if your wrists get sore to the point where you can't stand the pain. If you don't need them, don't use them, and don't be afraid to get rid of them if you find you can. Many of the top lifters in the world use some kind of wrist wrap, but not all of them. I don't like wrist wraps that are too bulky. I like them to be supportive but flexible. If you're somebody who has a problem keeping your hand closed on the bar when you catch your cleans on your shoulders, bulky wrist wraps might make the problem worse. Don't be afraid to experiment with different types of wraps and don't think you have to buy them only from some kind of weightlifting specialized company. Most of the wraps I've used in my career have been things I found at Sports Authority or Wal-Mart. And I personally hate using tape on my wrists. It's too restrictive and expensive for me, but some lifters like it.

TAPE ON HANDS OR FINGERS: Many lifters wrap tape around their fingers, or sometimes around the palms of their hands, if they're trying to protect a torn callous or simply for better grip. I used to tape my thumbs for every workout and meet, but I stopped doing it years ago and haven't noticed any difference. There's nothing wrong with using tape on your hands unless it interferes with your grip on the bar, which can happen if the tape is too stiff or bulky.

KNEE SLEEVES/WRAPS: My opinion on these is exactly the same as what I just stated about wrist wraps. Also, it's important to know that there's a difference between sleeves and wraps. Sleeves are solid tubes made of neoprene, nylon, or some other kind of material. Rehband knee sleeves have been really popular with weightlifters for several years. I've used them and I liked them, but I do think there's the potential for the sleeve to push your patella slightly out of position because of its tightness and bulk. Like I said, though, I had good experience with them. However, my favorite type of sleeve is something very thin. Basically, I'm talking about the type of sleeve that just provides a little warmth in the joint without really giving any major support. Obviously, these types of sleeves are very close to wearing nothing at all, but that's what I think you should be doing anyway. If you're relying on sleeves or wraps to help you stand up with your cleans, then your legs aren't strong enough. I hate it when weightlifters use knee wraps, but there are a few who do it. Hossein Rezazedeh used knee wraps, so it's not like they're all bad. They're rare though, because I think most lifters don't like the hassle of using them.

STRAPS: I think weightlifters should always use straps on assistance pulling movements (snatch pulls, clean pulls, snatch or clean deadlift), but that's it. The only reason you should wear straps on your actual snatches or cleans is if your hands are chewed up to the point where you almost can't grip the bar. When you see training hall videos of top international lifters, that's why they're using straps. They train fifteen times a week and their hands are shredded. But if there's nothing seriously wrong with your hands, you shouldn't use straps on the snatch or the clean. They're a crutch, and they can cause some problems if you're a competitive lifter. Also, wearing straps in the clean can lead to some serious wrist injuries if they compromise turnover speed. I got hurt pretty bad doing this once, and I've known a couple of other lifters who did too.

I think these opinions are probably close to most of the other lifters and coaches I've trained with over the years. There's a pretty common way we use this stuff, and this is it. However, the biggest thing to remember is that you should only use equipment if pain forces you to. If you don't need it, don't use it. And this goes especially for newcomers. Everybody should start with just using shoes, shorts, and a shirt, and they should stay that way for as long as possible. There's nothing more pitiful than seeing a newbie doing

50 kg back squats with a belt or knee wraps. If you can abstain from all of this stuff forever, then do it. Just use your best judgment.

Closing

I'll wrap this section up by simply restating the premise that your career as a master will be more successful if you pay attention to these things. I can absolutely 100% guarantee that. Some people ignore them. Hey, I get it. I was the king of ignoring this stuff when I was young. A fellow lifter I've known for over twenty years always shares the funny story of the first time he met me when I was 20 years old. I was in the living room of my house eating an entire plate of Orange Danish right before I went to the gym to train. That was how much I gave a damn about nutrition back then.

And I got away with it. Some people can get away with it for a long time. Other people think they're getting away with it because they're lifting big weights, but they still feel like hammered crap all the time and they're starting to consider hanging up their shoes. If changing your habits in the categories we just examined could extend your career to many more years of success, isn't it worth it? I know many of you are stubborn. Pack mules are stubborn too. That's why they only get used for menial labor and people whip the hell out of them. Do you want to be a pack mule in the weightlifting world, or would you rather be a champion thoroughbred racehorse?

Your call.

SECTION SIX

Resolution and Attitude

As we move towards the end of this thing, I want to come full circle and reconnect with a few of the concepts we talked about in the beginning. The introduction of this book was about mindset. The idea we've tried to build is that you'll only have success in the masters weightlifting game if you make the right decisions about your life and your career. The first decision is basic: choosing to take the plunge and engage in Olympic weightlifting in your older years. Following that, you'll have to make nonstop decisions about the way you train, the way you compete, how you treat your body, and a plethora of other areas that we've tried to give you some helpful input about.

However, the most important decision you'll have to continually make in your journey is simply to continue. This ain't gonna be easy, my friends. Setbacks will pop up frequently, and you'll have pain. There might be times when you consider throwing in the towel. Hell, other people might be openly telling you to give it up.

To address this, I want to tell you about a guy I know of. Incidentally, he's not even a weightlifter. His name is Ranulph Fiennes. He's a British explorer, born in 1944. At the time I'm writing this book, he's 70 years old. Fiennes is one of those guys who've been going on death-defying adventures around the globe for most of his life. You've heard about those dudes who climb Mount Everest, hike across frozen tundra... that kind of stuff, right? This guy is one of them. But he's not just your garden-variety explorer. A few years ago, I watched a documentary on him and it literally changed my outlook on several things, including my own life. Let me give you a few of his accomplishments:

- When he was 49, he became the first man to cross the Antarctic continent unsupported.
- When he was 56, he attempted to walk solo and unsupported to the North Pole. The expedition failed when his sled fell through a sheet of ice and he was plunged into freezing water. After he survived, he suffered severe frostbite to his hands and a doctor told him that his fingertips would have to be amputated. The doctor wanted to wait several months to do it, because he wanted as much healthy tissue as possible to grow around the frostbitten areas. Fiennes grew impatient over the following weeks, so he eventually just cut his fingertips off himself with a saw.
- When he was 59, he suffered a heart attack and had to go through double bypass surgery. Four months later, he ran seven marathons in seven days on seven different continents.
- When he was 65, he climbed Mount Everest.

I'm just mentioning the stunts he's pulled off in his later years, because obviously I want to make a point about the kind of amazing things that are possible in old age. Fiennes has been running around the planet and taking on insane challenges since the 1960s. If you look at what I listed above, you'll notice that these are the things he's done since he was around 50. The guy sawed his own fingers off because he was tired of waiting for a doctor to do it. He had a heart attack, and then ran seven marathons in one week just a few months later. He climbed Mount Everest at 65. To make a long story short, Ranulph Fiennes is one of the toughest SOBs I've ever heard of. Every time I read something about him, I'm in awe.

Think about the courage it would take to run seven marathons in a week. That's a more severe test of the human body than most people would even consider. Then think about doing it when you're 59 years old. Then…think about doing it four months after you've had a heart attack. Aside from the physical resiliency it would take to pull this off, can you imagine the bravery involved? Imagine putting your shoes on and stepping up to the starting line of those races. You would still have that heart attack in your mind. There's no way you would be able to fully block it out. In other words, you'd go into that race knowing that you're risking death. And I mean *really* risking death. Then you do it seven times in seven days.

Most people would shy away from this, without question. Ranulph Fiennes did it, and then he climbed Mount Everest six years later when he was 65. Once again, this was a challenge that involved mortal danger. Everest is the tallest mountain on Earth. People die trying to climb it. For crying out loud, 15 people died on it in 1996 alone. There's actually a section near the top of the mountain that's officially called "The Death Zone." The mental and physical toughness necessary to conquer this thing are extreme, and it's not something we normally associate with senior citizens. Old people are supposed to sit on their porch in a rocking chair and enjoy the golden years, right?

Anyway, back to that documentary I saw on Fiennes. A female interviewer was asking him questions about his life, which he answered with a very deadpan, calm voice. At one point, the interviewer was clearly astounded at the sheer resilience involved in his career, the determination and refusal to give up. She asked him, "Don't you ever think about quitting?" At that moment, Fiennes said something I'm never going to forget. His reply was, "Yes, sometimes you hear a voice in your head that tells you to give up. But you can't listen to it. The voice that tells you to quit must be treated with suspicion."

Brothers and sisters, that's the greatest quote I've ever heard. I went to my desk and wrote it down as soon as I heard it.

"The voice that tells you to quit must be treated with suspicion."

Let me tell you something about my own weightlifting career. Whenever I set up a training program for a competition, I create a document file on my computer to record all my workouts and make notes as the weeks roll forward. Some people like to write down their training in a book, but I prefer to do it on my computer. Whenever I start a new cycle, I put a heading at the top of it with the name of the meet, the date, and the location. It's a common practice I've been doing for several years. After I heard that quote from Ranulph Fiennes, I decided to start including it as part of the heading for all my competition programs. I'm going to copy & paste a few of these headings right here. These are taken directly from my personal training log.

TRAINING PROGRAM FOR
2012 AMERICAN MASTERS CHAMPIONSHIP
11/11/12, MONROVIA, CA

"The voice that tells you to quit must be treated with suspicion."

TRAINING PROGRAM FOR
2008 AMERICAN OPEN
12/7/08, CHANDLER, AZ

"The voice that tells you to quit must be treated with suspicion."

TRAINING PROGRAM FOR
2009 GARDEN STATE GAMES
6/27/09, MADISON, NJ

"The voice that tells you to quit must be treated with suspicion."

I've made this sentence a part of my life. In my opinion, it basically boils the journey of a weightlifter down to the bare essential truth. You WILL think about quitting occasionally. There's no way to sustain a long, arduous career without encountering some painful setbacks. When these setbacks hit us in the face, there's a moment when we imagine how much easier everything would be if we just walked away from all the stress and hardship. This is human instinct. You shouldn't feel cowardly or weak if you've heard the voice Fiennes was describing. We all hear it sooner or later.

However, the way you respond to the voice is what really matters. This quote tells us that the thought of quitting is a deceptive one. It's like being tempted by the Devil. When it first occurs to you how nice and easy it would be to give up the struggle, it sounds enticing. No more aches and pains. No more aggravation. No more pressure and worrying about your performance. No more days spent obsessing about your diet or the knot in your lower back. Hey, those things sound lovely.

But as I said, the voice is trying to trick you because what it's really telling you to do is abandon the thing you love the most. Even though weightlifting is tough on you, it's something you love. It gives you more happiness and fulfillment than most of the other things you've done in your life. The voice in your head wants you to throw it away. You're all intelligent people, so you understand what I'm driving towards.

Admittedly, it's important for us to acknowledge the fact that there *will* be a proper time for you to retire, at some point. The quote from Fiennes could be misinterpreted, causing people to think that there's never ever a suitable reason to call it quits. I don't think that's how we want to look at your career. There probably will come a time when it's right for you to step away. It's usually part of the process, unless you decide that you just want to pound away at this sport until you break in half or drop dead on the platform someday. And if that's the way you want it to play out, I respect that. I believe in free will, and everybody has the right to choose how they want to exit this world.

The point we're really trying to communicate is that you should quit for the right reasons, when it's the right time. You're trying to reach a moment when you're totally at peace with what you've done. It "feels right" to let it go. You've accomplished everything you wanted, or at least enough to give you a feeling of contentment and pride. You don't have regrets in your mind, at least not the kind that are going to plague you like a sickness for the rest of your life. You're looking at your body with intelligence and responsibility, understanding how you want to be able to live the rest of your life. If all these things come together and you have a clear sense of peace and happiness, maybe it's time to hang it up.

I've chosen to "never say never" in my weightlifting career. There have been time periods where I stepped away temporarily, but I've never declared any kind of permanent retirement from competition. I want to always leave the door open for a comeback. At this point in my life, I know I'm always going to get the itch again, sooner or later. I doubt if that's ever going to go away completely. So I continue training, regardless of whether I'm getting ready for a meet or not, and then I walk back into the fray when I'm ready. It's very important that you stay active. Don't ever walk away from everything entirely, because some form of exercise and physical activity will extend your life. It's good for you, competitive or not.

The bottom line, and the final thought of this book, is that your attitude is the secret ingredient in this whole shebang. Look at the life of Ranulph Fiennes. Read the words of all the great masters lifters who were kind enough to share their philosophies with us. Think about those world record lifts that have been put up by masters lifters. That's what this whole thing is about, brothers and sisters. Some of you might become champions. Others might never make a big splash as competitive Olympic lifters. But regardless of whether you win gold medals or not, choosing this sport as a part of your life can change everything about your time in this world. Trust me, you won't be the same person after you've taken the journey. Something inside you will be different. You'll be better than you were before, and it'll stay with you for the rest of your life. It's a tough road to travel, but that's why the payoff is so great. Best of luck to every single one of you.

Made in the USA
Coppell, TX
27 January 2020